The

NORTON MIX

NORTON
CUSTOM

W · W · NORTON & COMPANY · *New York* · *London*

The
NORTON MIX

A CUSTOM PUBLICATION

Readings on Language
and Literacy

W. W. Norton & Company has been independent since its founding in 1923, when William Warder Norton and Mary D. Herter Norton first published lectures delivered at the People's Institute, the adult education division of New York City's Cooper Union. The firm soon expanded its program beyond the Institute, publishing books by celebrated academics from America and abroad. By mid-century, the two major pillars of Norton's publishing program— trade books and college texts—were firmly established. In the 1950s, the Norton family transferred control of the company to its employees, and today—with a staff of four hundred and a comparable number of trade, college, and professional titles published each year— W. W. Norton & Company stands as the largest and oldest publishing house owned wholly by its employees.

Copyright © 2011 by W. W. Norton & Company, Inc.

Editor: Katie Hannah
Developmental editors: Mike Fleming and Erin Granville
Managing editor: Marian Johnson
Project editor: Melissa Atkin
Editorial assistant: Sophie Hagen
Production managers: Eric Pier-Hocking and Ashley Horna
Permissions editor: Nancy Rodwan
Photo permissions editor: Trish Marx
Designer: Toni Krass
Cover designs: Debra Morton-Hoyt
Emedia editor: Eileen Connell
Marketing manager: Scott Berzon
Proofreaders: Paulette McGee, Ben Reynolds
Composition: RR Donnelley
Manufacturing: RR Donnelley

ISBN-13 978-0-393-15744-4

W. W. Norton & Company, Inc., 500 Fifth Avenue, New York, N.Y. 10110
www.wwnorton.com
W. W. Norton & Company Ltd., Castle House, 75/76 Wells Street, London W1T 3QT

GENERAL EDITORS

ELIZABETH RODRIGUEZ KESSLER
COORDINATING EDITOR
University of Houston

JEFFREY ANDELORA
Mesa Community College

KATHARINE N. INGS
Manchester College

ANGELA L. JONES
Western Kentucky University

CHRISTOPHER KELLER
University of Texas–Pan American

WITH CONTRIBUTIONS FROM
CEDRIC BURROWS
University of Kansas

LORI CHASTAINE
Boise State University

MICHELLE L. CHESTER
Towson University

WANDA FRIES
Somerset Community College

HOLLY HASSEL
University of Wisconsin–Marathon County

BETH DINATALE JOHNSON
Ursuline College

Contents

Contents

MORTIMER J. ADLER ⎰ *How to Mark a Book*

MORTIMER J. ADLER (1902–2001), a native of New York City, dropped
out of school at fourteen, to embark on a career in journalism. He began taking night courses at Columbia University to develop his writing skills and
discovered a love of philosophy. By the late 1920s Adler was teaching at
Columbia while pursuing his doctorate and writing his first book, *Dialectic*
(1927). Along with Max Weismann, Adler founded The Center for the
Study of Great Ideas to investigate such philosophical questions as "What
ought we seek in life?" and "How ought we seek it?"

In "How to Mark a Book," Adler explains not only *how* to mark a book,
but also *why* we should mark our books. Adler uses a range of rhetorical
strategies—process analysis, description, definition, division and classification, and exemplification—to develop his ideas. Real ownership of books,
Adler advises, comes from truly possessing the ideas, not just the pages,
between the covers, and the point of reading is not to get through books but
to get them through you.

YOU KNOW YOU HAVE TO read "between the lines" to get the most out
of anything. I want to persuade you to do something equally important
in the course of your reading. I want to persuade you to write between
the lines. Unless you do, you are not likely to do the most efficient kind
of reading.

I contend, quite bluntly, that marking up a book is not an act of mutilation but of love. You shouldn't mark up a book which isn't yours.

Librarians (or your friends) who lend you books expect you to keep

"How to Mark a Book" by Mortimer Adler. Reprinted by permission of the Estate of
Mortimer Adler.

them clean, and you should. If you decide that I am right about the usefulness of marking books, you will have to buy them. Most of the world's great books are available today, in reprint editions.

There are two ways in which one can own a book. The first is the property right you establish by paying for it, just as you pay for clothes and furniture. But this act of purchase is only the prelude to possession. Full ownership comes only when you have made it a part of yourself, and the best way to make yourself a part of it is by writing in it. An illustration may make the point clear. You buy a beefsteak and transfer it from the butcher's icebox to your own. But you do not own the beefsteak in the most important sense until you consume it and get it into your bloodstream. I am arguing that books, too, must be absorbed in your bloodstream to do you any good.

Confusion about what it means to "own" a book leads people to a 5
false reverence for paper, binding, and type—a respect for the physical thing—the craft of the printer rather than the genius of the author. They forget that it is possible for a man to acquire the idea, to possess the beauty, which a great book contains, without staking his claim by pasting his bookplate inside the cover. Having a fine library doesn't prove that its owner has a mind enriched by books; it proves nothing more than that he, his father, or his wife, was rich enough to buy them.

There are three kinds of book owners. The first has all the standard sets and best sellers—unread, untouched. (This deluded individual owns woodpulp and ink, not books.) The second has a great many books—a few of them read through, most of them dipped into, but all of them as clean and shiny as the day they were bought. (This person would probably like to make books his own, but is restrained by a false respect for their physical appearance.) The third has a few books or many—every one of them dog-eared and dilapidated, shaken and loosened by continual use, marked and scribbled in from front to back. (This man owns books.)

Is it false respect, you may ask, to preserve intact and unblemished a beautifully printed book, an elegantly bound edition? Of course not. I'd no more scribble all over a first edition of *Paradise Lost* than I'd give my baby a set of crayons and an original Rembrandt. I wouldn't mark up a painting or a statue. Its soul, so to speak, is inseparable from its body. And the beauty of a rare edition or of a richly manufactured volume is like that of a painting or a statue.

But the soul of a book "can" be separate from its body. A book is more like the score of a piece of music than it is like a painting. No great musician confuses a symphony with the printed sheets of music. Arturo Toscanini reveres Brahms,[1] but Toscanini's score of the G minor Symphony is so thoroughly marked up that no one but the maestro himself can read it. The reason why a great conductor makes notations on his musical scores—marks them up again and again each time he returns to study them—is the reason why you should mark your books. If your respect for magnificent binding or typography gets in the way, buy yourself a cheap edition and pay your respects to the author.

Why is marking up a book indispensable to reading? First, it keeps you awake. (And I don't mean merely conscious; I mean awake.) In the second place, reading, if it is active, is thinking, and thinking tends to express itself in words, spoken or written. The marked book is usually the thought-through book. Finally, writing helps you remember the thoughts you had, or the thoughts the author expressed. Let me develop these three points.

If reading is to accomplish anything more than passing time, it must 10 be active. You can't let your eyes glide across the lines of a book and come up with an understanding of what you have read. Now an ordinary piece of light fiction, like, say, *Gone With the Wind*,[2] doesn't require the most active kind of reading. The books you read for pleasure can be read in a state of relaxation, and nothing is lost. But a great book, rich in ideas and beauty, a book that raises and tries to answer great fundamental questions, demands the most active reading of which you are capable. You don't absorb the ideas of John Dewey the way you absorb the crooning of Mr. Vallée.[3] You have reach for them. That you cannot do while you're asleep.

[1]Arturo Toscanini (1867–1957), Italian musician considered one of history's greatest orchestral conductors; Johannes Brahms (1833–97), German composer of the Romantic era.

[2]Popular novel (1937) of the Civil War by Margaret Mitchell (1900–49).

[3]John Dewey (1859–1952), American philosopher and educational reformer; Rudy Vallée (1901–86), American singer and bandleader.

If, when you've finished reading a book, the pages are filled with your notes, you know that you read actively. The most famous "active" reader of great books I know is President Hutchins,[4] of the University of Chicago. He also has the hardest schedule of business activities of any man I know. He invariably reads with a pencil, and sometimes, when he picks up a book and pencil in the evening, he finds himself, instead of making intelligent notes, drawing what he calls "caviar factories" on the margins. When that happens, he puts the book down. He knows he's too tired to read, and he's just wasting time.

But, you may ask, why is writing necessary? Well, the physical act of writing, with your own hand, brings words and sentences more sharply before your mind and preserves them better in your memory. To set down your reaction to important words and sentences you have read, and the questions they have raised in your mind, is to preserve those reactions and sharpen those questions.

Even if you wrote on a scratch pad, and threw the paper away when you had finished writing, your grasp of the book would be surer. But you don't have to throw the paper away. The margins (top and bottom as well as side), the end-papers, the very space between the lines, are all available. They aren't sacred. And, best of all, your marks and notes become an integral part of the book and stay there forever. You can pick up the book the following week or year, and there are all your points of agreement, disagreement, doubt, and inquiry. It's like resuming an interrupted conversation with the advantage of being able to pick up where you left off.

And that is exactly what reading a book should be: a conversation between you and the author. Presumably he knows more about the subject than you do; naturally, you'll have the proper humility as you approach him. But don't let anybody tell you that a reader is supposed to be solely on the receiving end. Understanding is a two-way operation; learning doesn't consist in being an empty receptacle. The learner has to question himself and question the teacher. He even has to argue with the teacher, once he understands what the teacher is say-

---

[4]Robert Hutchins (1899–1977), educational philosopher and president of the University of Chicago, where he hired Mortimer Adler as a professor of the philosophy of law.

ing. And marking a book is literally an expression of differences, or agreements of opinion, with the author.

There are all kinds of devices for marking a book intelligently and 15 fruitfully. Here's the way I do it:

- **Underlining (or highlighting):** of major points, of important or forceful statements.

- **Vertical lines at the margin:** to emphasize a statement already underlined.

- **Star, asterisk, or other doo-dad at the margin:** to be used sparingly, to emphasize the ten or twenty most important statements in the book. (You may want to fold the bottom corner of each page on which you use such marks. It won't hurt the sturdy paper on which most modern books are printed, and you will be able take the book off the shelf at any time and, by opening it at the folded-corner page, refresh your recollection of the book.)

- **Numbers in the margin:** to indicate the sequence of points the author makes in developing a single argument.

- **Numbers of other pages in the margin:** to indicate where else in the book the author made points relevant to the point marked; to tie up the ideas in a book, which, though they may be separated by many pages, belong together.

- **Circling or highlighting of key words or phrases.**

- **Writing in the margin, or at the top or bottom of the page:** for the sake of recording questions (and perhaps answers) which a passage raised in your mind; reducing a complicated discussion to a simple statement; recording the sequence of major points right through the books. I use the end-papers at the back of the book to make a personal index of the author's points in the order of their appearance.

The front end-papers are to me the most important. Some people reserve them for a fancy bookplate. I reserve them for fancy thinking.

After I have finished reading the book and making my personal index on the back end-papers, I turn to the front and try to outline the book, not page by page or point by point (I've already done that at the back), but as an integrated structure, with a basic unity and an order of parts. This outline is, to me, the measure of my understanding of the work.

If you're a die-hard anti-book-marker, you may object that the margins, the space between the lines, and the end-papers don't give you room enough. All right. How about using a scratch pad slightly smaller than the page-size of the book—so that the edges of the sheets won't protrude? Make your index, outlines, and even your notes on the pad, and then insert these sheets permanently inside the front and back covers of the book.

Or, you may say that this business of marking books is going to slow up your reading. It probably will. That's one of the reasons for doing it. Most of us have been taken in by the notion that speed of reading is a measure of our intelligence. There is no such thing as the right speed for intelligent reading. Some things should be read quickly and effortlessly and some should be read slowly and even laboriously. The sign of intelligence in reading is the ability to read different things differently according to their worth. In the case of good books, the point is not to see how many of them you can get through, but rather how many can get through you—how many you can make your own. A few friends are better than a thousand acquaintances. If this be your aim, as it should be, you will not be impatient if it takes more time and effort to read a great book than it does a newspaper.

You may have one final objection to marking books. You can't lend them to your friends because nobody else can read them without being distracted by your notes. Furthermore, you won't want to lend them because a marked copy is kind of intellectual diary, and lending it is almost like giving your mind away.

If your friend wishes to read your *Plutarch's Lives, Shakespeare,* or 20 *The Federalist Papers,* tell him gently but firmly to buy a copy. You will lend him your car or your coat—but your books are as much a part of you as your head or your heart.

6

STUDY QUESTIONS

1. Why does Adler advise against lending books to friends? What comparison does he use to explore the idea of owning a book, and how effective is it?

2. Numbering items in an essay is a rhetorical technique that can help guide readers through the development of an idea. Adler uses this TRANSITION technique several times in his article. Find these passages and explain what he enumerates. Does the strategy help you to follow his reasoning? Why or why not?

3. The "how to" in Adler's title indicates that he will present a process. Look carefully for the way Adler structures the process of marking a book. Find each step in the process and number them in the order in which they occur. Are there enough to guide someone through the process? Explain.

4. *For Writing.* Adler clearly cares very much about reading books and absorbing their content. Choose an activity for which you have a similar passion, and write a PROCESS ANALYSIS essay describing how best to enjoy that activity. Reread Adler's essay and make sure your essay covers all relevant aspects of participating in the activity, answers possible objections to doing it your way, and provides signposts and transitions for your reader to follow, as Adler's does.

{ *How to Tame a Wild Tongue*

GLORIA ANZALDÚA (1942–2004), a Chicana lesbian feminist, is a well-known early female voice in Chicana writing. Her first work, *This Bridge Called My Back* (1981), was co-authored with Cherríe Moraga. Her next book, *Borderlands / La Frontera: The New Mestiza* (1987) called attention not only to the difficulties she encountered growing up in the Rio Grande Valley of Texas, but also to the hardships faced by other women living along the U.S./Mexican border. Anzaldúa's other works include *Making Face, Making Soul / Haciendo Caras* (1990) and *Prietita and the Ghost Woman* (1996), a book for children.

In "How to Tame a Wild Tongue," an essay from *Borderlands*, Anzaldúa explores the linguistic borders between Mexico and the United States and the "border tongues" and ethnic identities that cross them. Her frequent use of Spanish will challenge those who do not read the language to find a dictionary or a Spanish speaker in order to discover the meaning not only of the words but also of the deeper ideas and emotions that English sometimes cannot convey for her. As you read, consider the reasons Anzaldúa might have for insisting that editors not translate her Spanish phrases for English readers. In this bilingual fashion, Anzaldúa allows her "wild tongue" to express itself fully and without constraint.

"WE'RE GOING TO HAVE TO control your tongue," the dentist says, pulling out all the metal from my mouth. Silver bits plop and tinkle into the basin. My mouth is a motherlode.

The dentist is cleaning out my roots. I get a whiff of the stench when I gasp. "I can't cap that tooth yet, yu're still draining," he says.

"We're going to have to do something about your tongue," I hear the anger rising in his voice. My tongue keeps pushing out the wads of cotton, pushing back the drills, the long thin needles. "I've never seen anything as strong or as stubborn," he says. And I think, how do you tame a wild tongue, train it to be quiet, how do you bridle and saddle it? How do you make it lie down?

> *"Who is to say that robbing a people of its language is less violent than war?"*
>
> —RAY GWYN SMITH[1]

I remember being caught speaking Spanish at recess—that was good for three licks on the knuckles with a sharp ruler. I remember being sent to the corner of the classroom for "talking back" to the Anglo teacher when all I was trying to do was tell her how to pronounce my name. "If you want to be American, speak 'American.' If you don't like it, go back to Mexico where you belong."

"I want you to speak English. *Pa'hallar buen trabajo tienes que saber*   5
hablar el inglés bien. Qué vale toda tu educación si todavía hablas inglés con un 'accent,' " my mother would say, mortified that I spoke English like a Mexican. At Pan American University, I, and all Chicano students were required to take two speech classes. Their purpose: to get rid of our accents.

Attacks on one's form of expression with the intent to censor are a violation of the First Amendment. *El Anglo con cara de inocente nos arrancó la lengua.* Wild tongues can't be tamed, they can only be cut out.

OVERCOMING THE TRADITION OF SILENCE

> *Ahogadas, escupimos el oscuro.*
> *Peleando con nuestra propia sombra*
> *el silencio nos sepulta.*

En boca cerrada no entran moscas. "Flies don't enter a closed mouth" is a saying I kept hearing when I was a child. *Ser habladora* was to be

---

[1]Ray Gwyn Smith, *Moorland Is Cold Country*, unpublished book.

a gossip and a liar, to talk too much. *Muchachitas bien criadas,* well-bred girls don't answer back. *Es una falta de respeto* to talk back to one's mother or father. I remember one of the sins I'd recite to the priest in the confession box the few times I went to confession: talking back to my mother, *hablar pa' 'trás, repelar. Hocicona, repelona, chismosa,* having a big mouth, questioning, carrying tales are all signs of being *mal criada.* In my culture they are all words that are derogatory if applied to women—I've never heard them applied to men.

The first time I heard two women, a Puerto Rican and a Cuban, say the word *"nosotras,"* I was shocked. I had not known the word existed. Chicanas use *nosotros* whether we're male or female. We are robbed of our female being by the masculine plural. Language is a male discourse.

> And our tongues have become
> dry   the wilderness has
> dried out our tongues   and
> we have forgotten speech.
> —IRENA KLEPFISZ[2]

Even our own people, other Spanish speakers *nos quieren poner candados en la boca.* They would hold us back with their bag of *reglas de academia.*

OYÉ COMO LADRA: EL LENGUAJE DE LA FRONTERA

Quien tiene boca se equivoca.
—MEXICAN SAYING

"*Pocho,* cultural traitor, you're speaking the oppressor's language by   10
speaking English, you're ruining the Spanish language," I have been accused by various Latinos and Latinas. Chicano Spanish is considered by the purist and by most Latinos deficient, a mutilation of Spanish.

[2]Irena Klepfisz, "*Di rayze aheym/*The Journey Home," in *The Tribe of Dina: A Jewish Women's Anthology,* Melanie Kaye/Kantrowitz and Irena Klepfisz, eds. (Montpelier, VT: Sinister Wisdom Books, 1986), 49.

But Chicano Spanish is a border tongue which developed naturally. Change, *evolución, enriquecimiento de palabras nuevas por invención o adopción* have created variants of Chicano Spanish, *un nuevo lenguaje. Un lenguaje que corresponde a un modo de vivir.* Chicano Spanish is not incorrect, it is a living language.

For a people who are neither Spanish nor live in a country in which Spanish is the first language; for a people who live in a country in which English is the reigning tongue but who are not Anglo; for a people who cannot entirely identify with either standard (formal, Castillian) Spanish nor standard English, what recourse is left to them but to create their own language? A language which they can connect their identity to, one capable of communicating the realities and values true to themselves—a language with terms that are neither *español ni inglés,* but both. We speak a patois, a forked tongue, a variation of two languages.

Chicano Spanish sprang out of the Chicanos' need to identify ourselves as a distinct people. We needed a language with which we could communicate with ourselves, a secret language. For some of us, language is a homeland closer than the Southwest—for many Chicanos today live in the Midwest and the East. And because we are a complex, heterogeneous people, we speak many languages. Some of the languages we speak are:

1. Standard English
2. Working-class and slang English
3. Standard Spanish
4. Standard Mexican Spanish
5. North Mexican Spanish dialect
6. Chicano Spanish (Texas, New Mexico, Arizona and California have regional variations)
7. Tex-Mex
8. *Pachuco* (called *caló*)

My "home" tongues are the languages I speak with my sister and brothers, with my friends. They are the last five listed, with 6 and 7 being closest to my heart. From school, the media and job situations, I've picked up standard and working class English. From Mamagrande Locha and from reading Spanish and Mexican literature, I've picked up Standard Spanish and Standard Mexican Spanish. From *los recién llega-*

dos, Mexican immigrants, and *braceros,* I learned the North Mexican dialect. With Mexicans I'll try to speak either Standard Mexican Spanish or the North Mexican dialect. From my parents and Chicanos living in the Valley, I picked up Chicano Texas Spanish, and I speak it with my mom, younger brother (who married a Mexican and who rarely mixes Spanish with English), aunts and older relatives.

With Chicanas from *Nuevo México* or *Arizona* I will speak Chicano 15 Spanish a little, but often they don't undrstand what I'm saying. With most California Chicanas I speak entirely in English (unless I forget). When I first moved to San Francisco, I'd rattle off something in Spanish, unintentionally embarrassing them. Often it is only with another Chicana *tejana* that I can talk freely.

Words distorted by English are known as anglicisms or *pochismos.* The *pocho* is an anglicized Mexican or American of Mexican origin who speaks Spanish with an accent characteristic of North Americans and who distorts and reconstructs the language according to the influence of English.[3] Tex-Mex, or Spanglish, comes most naturally to me. I may switch back and forth from English to Spanish in the same sentence or in the same word. With my sister and my brother Nune and with Chicano *tejano* contemporaries I speak in Tex-Mex.

From kids and people my own age I picked up *Pachuco. Pachuco* (the language of the zoot suiters) is a language of rebellion, both against Standard Spanish and Standard English. It is a secret language. Adults of the culture and outsiders cannot understand it. It is mad up of slang words from both English and Spanish. *Ruca* means girl or women, *vato* means guy or dude, *chale* means no, *simón* means yes, *churo* is sure, talk is *periquiar, pigionear* means petting, *que gacho* means how nerdy, *ponte águila* means watch out, death is called *la pelona.* Through lack of practice and not having others who can speak it, I've lost most of the *Pachuco* tongue.

[3]R. C. Ortega *Dialectología Del Barrio*, trans. Hortencia S. Alwan (Los Angeles, CA: R. C. Ortega Publisher & Bookseller, 1977), 132.

CHICANO SPANISH

Chicanos, after 250 years of Spanish/Anglo colonization have developed significant differences in the Spanish we speak. We collapse two adjacent vowels into a single syllable and sometimes shift the stress in certain words such as *maíz/maiz, cohete/cuete.* We leave out certain consonants when they appear between vowels: *lado/lao, mojado/mojao.* Chicanos from South Texas pronounce *f* as *j* as in *jue (fue).* Chicanos use "archaisms," words that are no longer in the Spanish language, words that have been evolved out. We say *semos, truje, haiga, ansina,* and *naiden.* We retain the "archaic" *j,* as in *jalar,* that derives from an earlier *h,* (the French *halar* or the Germanic *halon* which was lost to standard Spanish in the 16th century), but which is still found in several regional dialects such as the one spoken in South Texas. (Due to geography, Chicanos from the Valley of South Texas were cut off linguistically from other Spanish speakers. We tend to use words that the Spaniards brought over from Medieval Spain. The majority of the Spanish colonizers in Mexico and the Southwest came from Extremadura[4]—Hernán Cortés was one of them—and Andalucía. Andalucians pronounce *ll* like a *y,* and their *d*'s tend to be absorbed by adjacent vowels: *tirado* becomes *tirao.* They brought *el lenguaje popular, dialectos y regionalismos.*[5])

Chicanos and other Spanish speakers also shift *ll* to *y* and *z* to *s.*[6] We leave out initial syllables, saying *tar* for *estar, toy* for *estoy, hora* for *ahora* (*cubanos* and *puertorriqueños* also leave out initial letters of some words.) We also leave out the final syllable such as *pa* for *para.* The intervocalic *y,* the *ll* as in *tortilla, ella, botella,* gets replaced by *tortia* or *tortiya, ea, botea.* We add an additional syllable at the beginning of certain words: *atocar* for *tocar, agastar* for *gastar.* Sometimes we'll

[4]Large region of southern Spain. *Hernán Cortés*: Spanish conquistador (1485–1547) who defeated the Aztec empire and claimed Mexico for Spain. [Ed.]
[5]Eduardo Hernandéz-Chávez, Andrew D. Cohen, and Anthony F. Beltramo, *El Lenguaje de Chicanos: Regional and Social Characteristics of Language Used by Mexican Americans* (Arlington, VA: Center for Applied Linguistics, 1975), 39.
[6]Hernandéz-Chávez, xvii.

say *lavaste las vacijas,* other times *lavates* (substituting the *ates* verb endings for the *aste*).

We use angliciams, words borrowed from English: *bola* from ball,   20
carpeta from carpet, *máchina de lavar* (instead of *lavadora*) from washing machine. Tex-Mex argot, created by adding a Spanish sound at the beginning or end of an English word such as *cookiar* for cook, *watchar* for watch, *parkiar* for park, and *rapiar* for rape, is the result of the pressures on Spanish speakers to adapt to English.

We don't use the word *vosotros/as* or its accompanying verb form. We don't say *claro* (to mean yes), *imagínate,* or *me emociona,* unless we picked up Spanish from Latinas[7], out of a book, or in a classroom. Other Spanish-speaking groups are going through the same, or similar, development in their Spanish.

LINGUISTIC TERRORISM

> *Deslenguadas. Somos los del español deficiente. We are your linguistic nightmare, your linguistic aberration, your linguistic* mestizaje, *the subject of your* burla. *Because we speak with tongues of fire we are culturally crucified. Racially, culturally and linguistically* somos huérfanos—*we speak an orphan tongue.*

Chicanas who grew up speaking Chicano Spanish have internalized the belief that we speak poor Spanish. It is illegitimate, a bastard language. And because we internalize how our language has been used against us by the dominant culture, we use our language differences against each other.

Chicana feminists often skirt around each other with suspicion and hesitation. For the longest time I couldn't figure it out. Then it dawned on me. To be close to another Chicana is like looking into the mirror. We are afraid of what we'll see there. *Pena.* Shame. Low estimation of self. In childhood we are told that our language is wrong. Repeated attacks on our native tongue diminish our sense of self. The attacks continue throughout our lives.

---

[7]That is, natives of Central and South America. [Ed.]

Chicanas feel uncomfortable talking in Spanish to Latinas, afraid of their censure. Their language was not outlawed in their countries. They had a whole lifetime of being immersed in their native tongue; generations, centuries in which Spanish was a first language, taught in school, heard on radio and TV, and read in the newspaper.

If a person, Chicana or Latina, has a low estimation of my native [25] tongue, she also has a low estimation of me. Often with *mexicanas y latinas* we'll speak English as a neutral language. Even among Chicanas we tend to speak English at parties or conferences. Yet, at the same time, we're afraid the other will think we're *agringadas* because we don't speak Chicano Spanish. We oppress each other trying to out-Chicano each other, vying to be the "real" Chicanas, to speak like Chicanos. There is no one Chicano language just as there is no one Chicano experience. A monolingual Chicana whose first language is English or Spanish is just as much a Chicana as one who speaks several variants of Spanish. A Chicana from Michigan or Chicago or Detroit is just as much a Chicana as one from the Southwest. Chicano Spanish is as diverse linguistically as it is regionally.

By the end of this century, Spanish speakers will comprise the biggest minority group in the U.S., a country where students in high schools and colleges are encouraged to take French classes because French is considered more "cultured." But for a language to remain alive it must be used.[8] By the end of this century English, and not Spanish, will be the mother tongue of most Chicanos and Latinos.

So, if you want to really hurt me, talk badly about my language. Ethnic identity is twin skin to linguistic identity—I am my language. Until I can take pride in my language, I cannot take pride in myself. Until I can accept as legitimate Chicano Texas Spanish, Tex-Mex and all the other languages I speak, I cannot accept the legitimacy of myself. Until I am free to write bilingually and to switch codes without having always to translate, while I still have to speak English or Spanish when I would rather speak Spanglish, and as long as I have to accommodate the English

---

[8]Irena Klepfisz, "Secular Jewish Identity: Yidishkayt in America," in *The Tribe of Dina*, Kaye/Kantrowitz and Klepfisz, eds., 43.

speakers rather than having them accommodate me, my tongue will be illegitimate.

I will no longer be made to feel ashamed of existing. I will have my voice: Indian, Spanish, white. I will have my serpent's tongue—my woman's voice, my sexual voice, my poet's voice. I will overcome the tradition of silence.

> *My fingers*
> *move sly against your palm.*
> *Like women everywhere, we speak in code. . . .*
> —MELANIE KAYE/KANTROWITZ[9]

"VISTAS," CORRIDOS, Y COMIDA: MY NATIVE TONGUE

In the 1960s, I read my first Chicano novel. It was *City of Night* by John Rechy, a gay Texan, son of a Scottish father and a Mexican mother. For days I walked around in stunned amazement that a Chicano could write and could get published. When I read *I Am Joaquín*[1] I was surprised to see a bilingual book by a Chicano in print. When I saw poetry written in Tex-Mex for the first time, a feeling of pure joy flashed through me. I felt like we really existed as a people. In 1971, when I started teaching High School English to Chicano students, I tried to supplement the required texts with works by Chicanos, only to be reprimanded and forbidden to do so by the principal. He claimed that I was supposed to teach "American" and English literature. At the risk of being fired, I swore my students to secrecy and slipped in Chicano short stories, poems, a play. In graduate school, while working toward a Ph.D., I had to "argue" with one advisor after the other, semester after semester, before I was allowed to make Chicano literature an area of focus.

Even before I read books by Chicanos or Mexicans, it was the 30

---

[9]Melanie Kaye/Kantrowitz, "Sign," in *We Speak in Code: Poems and Other Writings* (Pittsburgh, PA: Motheroot Publications, Inc., 1980), 85.
[1]Rodolfo Gonzales, *I Am Joaquín/Yo Soy Joaquín* (New York, NY: Bantam Books, 1972). It was first published in 1967.

Mexican movies I saw at the drive-in—the Thursday night special of $1.00 a carload—that gave me a sense of belonging. *"Vámonos a las vistas,"* my mother would call out and we'd all—grandmother, brothers, sister and cousins—squeeze into the car. We'd wolf down cheese and bologna white bread sandwiches while watching Pedro Infante in melodramatic tear-jerkers like *Nosotros los pobres,* the first "real" Mexican movie (that was not an imitation of European movies). I remember seeing *Cuando los hijos se van* and surmising that all Mexican movies played up the love a mother has for her children and what ungrateful sons and daughters suffer when they are not devoted to their mothers. I remember the singing-type "westerns" of Jorge Negrete and Miguel Aceves Mejía. When watching Mexican movies, I felt a sense of homecoming as well as alienation. People who were to amount to something didn't go to Mexican movies, or *bailes* or tune their radios to *bolero, rancherita,* and *corrido* music.

The whole time I was growing up, there was *norteño* music sometimes called North Mexican border music, or Tex-Mex music, or Chicano music, or *cantina* (bar) music. I grew up listening to *conjuntos,* three- or four-piece bands made up of folk musicians playing guitar, *bajo sexto,* drums and button accordion, which Chicanos had borrowed from the German immigrants who had come to Central Texas and Mexico to farm and build breweries. In the Rio Grande Valley, Steve Jordan and Little Joe Hernández were popular, and Flaco Jiménez was the accordion king. The rhythms of Tex-Mex music are those of the polka, also adapted from the Germans, who in turn had borrowed the polka from the Czechs and Bohemians. 35

I remember the hot, sultry evenings when *corridos*—songs of love and death on the Texas-Mexican borderlands—reverberated out of cheap amplifiers from the local *cantinas* and wafted in through my bedroom window.

Corridos first became widely used along the South Texas/Mexican border during the early conflict between Chicanos and Anglos. The *corridos* are usually about Mexican heroes who do valiant deeds against the Anglo oppressors. Pancho Villa's song, *"La cucaracha,"* is the most famous one. *Corridos* of John F. Kennedy and hsi death are still very popular in the Valley. Older Chicanos remember Lydia Mendoza, one of the great border *corrido* singers who was called *la Gloria de Tejas.* Her "*El tango negro,*" sung during the Great Depression, made her a singer of the people. The everpresent *corridos* narrated one hundred years of border history, bringing news of events as well as entertaining. These folk musicians and folk songs are our chief cultural mythmakers, and they made our hard lives seem bearable.

I grew up feeling ambivalent about our music. Country-western and rock-and-roll had more status. In the 50s and 60s, for the slightly educated and *agringado* Chicanos, there existed a sense of shame at being caught listening to our music. Yet I couldn't stop my feet from thumping to the music, could not stop humming the words, nor hide from myself the exhilaration I felt when I heard it.

There are more subtle ways that we internalize identification, espe- 35 cially in the forms of images and emotions. For me food and certain smells are tied to my identity, to my homeland. Woodsmoke curling up to an immense blue sky; woodsmoke perfuming my grandmother's clothes, her skin. The stench of cow manure and the yellow patches on the ground; the crack of a .22 rifle and the reek of cordite. Homemade white cheese sizzling in a pan, melting inside a folded *tortilla.* My sister Hilda's hot, spicy *menudo, chile colorado* making it deep red, pieces of *panza* and hominy floating on top. My brother Carito barbecuing *fajitas* in the backyard. Even now and 3,000 miles away, I can see my mother spicing the ground beef, pork and venison with *chile.* My mouth salivates at the thought of the hot steaming *tamales* I would be eating if I were home.

SI LE PREGUNTAS A MI MAMÁ, "¿QUÉ ERES?"

> "*Identity is the essential core of who we are as individuals, the conscious experience of the self inside.*"
>
> —KAUFMAN[2]

---

[2]Kaufman, 68.

Nosotros los Chicanos straddle the borderlands. On one side of us, we are constantly exposed to the Spanish of the Mexicans, on the other side we hear the Anglos' incessant clamoring so that we forget our language. Among ourselves we don't say *nosotros los americanos, o nosotros los españoles, o nosotros los hispanos.* We say *nosotros los mexicanos* (by *mexicanos* we do not mean citizens of Mexico; we do not mean a national identity, but a racial one). We distinguish between *mexicanos del otro lado* and *mexicanos de este lado.* Deep in our hearts we believe that being Mexican has nothing to do with which country one lives in. Being Mexican is a state of soul—not one of mind, not one of citizenship. Neither eagle nor serpent, but both. And like the ocean, neither animal respects borders.

> Dime con quien andas y te diré quien eres. *(Tell me who your friends are and I'll tell you who you are.)*
> —MEXICAN SAYING

Si le preguntas a mi mamá, "¿Qué eres?" te dirá, "Soy mexicana." My brothers and sister say the same. I sometimes will answer *"soy mexicana"* and at others will say *"soy Chicana" o "soy tejana."* But I identified as *"Raza"* before I ever identified as *"mexicana"* or "Chicana."

As a culture, we call ourselves Spanish when referring to ourselves as a linguistic group and when copping out. It is then that we forget our predominant Indian genes. We are 70 to 80% Indian.[3] We call ourselves Hispanic[4] or Spanish-American or Latin American or Latin when linking ourselves to other Spanish-speaking peoples of the Western hemisphere and when copping out. We call ourselves Mexican-American[5] to signify we are neither Mexican nor American, but more the noun "American" than the adjective "Mexican" (and when copping out).

Chicanos and other people of color suffer economically for not

---

[3]Chávez, 88–90.
[4]"Hispanic" is derived from *Hispanis (España,* a name given to the Iberian Peninsula in ancient times when it was a part of the Roman Empire) and is a term designated by the U.S. government to make it easier to handle us on paper.
[5]The treaty of Guadalupe Hidalgo created the Mexican-American in 1848.

acculturating. This voluntary (yet forced) alienation makes for psychological conflict, a kind of dual identity—we don't identify with the Anglo-American cultural values and we don't totally identify with the Mexican cultural values. We are a synergy of two cultures with various degrees of Mexicanness or Angloness. I have so internalized the borderland conflict that sometimes I feel like one cancels out the other and we are zero, nothing, no one. *A veces no soy nada ni nadie. Pero hasta cuando no lo soy, lo soy.*

When not copping out, when we know we are more than nothing, 40 we call ourselves Mexican, referring to race and ancestry; *mestizo* when affirming both our Indian and Spanish (but we hardly ever own our Black ancestry); Chicano when referring to a politically aware people born and/or raised in the U.S.; *Raza* when referring to Chicanos; *tejanos* when we are Chicanos from Texas.

Chicanos did not know we were a people until 1965 when Cesar Chavez and the farmworkers united and *I Am Joaquín* was published and *la Raza Unida* party was formed in Texas. With that recognition, we became a distinct people. Something momentous happened to the Chicano soul—we became aware of our reality and acquired a name and a language (Chicano Spanish) that reflected that reality. Now that we had a name, some of the fragmented pieces began to fall together— who we were, what we were, how we had evolved. We began to get glimpses of what we might eventually become.

Yet the struggle of identities continues, the struggle of borders is our reality still. One day the inner struggle will cease and a true integration take place. In the meantime, *tenemos que hacerla lucha, ¿Quién está protegiendo los ranchos de mi gente? ¿Quién está tratando de cerrar la fisura entre la india y el blanco en nuestra sangre? El Chicano, sí, el Chicano que anda como un ladron en su propia casa.*

Los Chicanos how patient we seem, how very patient. There is the quiet of the Indian about us.[6] We know how to survive. When other

---

[6]Anglos, in order to alleviate their guilt for dispossessing the Chicano, stressed the Spanish part of us and perpetrated the myth of the Spanish Southwest. We have accepted the fiction that we are Hispanic, that is Spanish, in order to accommoadate ourselves to the dominant culture and its abhorrence of Indians. Chávez, 88–91.

races have given up their tongue, we've kept ours. We know what it is to live under the hammer blow of the dominant *norteamericano* culture. But more than we count the blows, we count the days the weeks the years the centuries the eons until the white laws and commerce and customs will rot in the deserts they've created, lie bleached. *Humildes* yet proud, *quietos* yet wild, *nosotros los mexicanos*-Chicanos will walk by the crumbling ashes as we go about our business. Stubborn, persevering, impenetrable as stone, yet possessing a malleability that renders us unbreakable, we, the *mestizas* and *mestizos,* will remain.

STUDY QUESTIONS

1. What is the "Pachuco" language? Explain how the various languages Anzaldúa discusses are related to the "wild tongue" reference in the title of her essay.

2. One of the RHETORICAL STRATEGIES Anzaldúa uses in her essay is DEFINITION, to ensure that the reader understands how the author will use a given term. Furthermore, the definition may be extended and clarified with examples. Find two examples of Anzaldúa's use of definition in this essay and explain how each functions in the overall essay.

3. Anzaldúa specified that when her work is reprinted, no footnotes be added to translate the Spanish and other foreign words and phrases she uses. What effect does this practice have on you as a reader? What do you think Anzaldúa is trying to achieve?

4. *For Writing.* Many speakers of other languages find it difficult to solely express themselves in English because it can be difficult to find the English word whose connotations best suit its meaning. For example, the Spanish words *cariño* and *amor* both mean *love* but are used for different situations. Write a PERSONAL NARRATIVE about an important situation in your life when it seemed as though English—or any other language—lacked the right words to convey effectively what you wanted to say.

NAOMI S. BARON $\Big\{$ *Killing the Written Word by Snippets*

NAOMI S. BARON (b. 1946), professor of linguistics at American University, has written extensively on language, communication, and technology. She earned her BA in American and English literature at Brandeis University and her PhD in linguistics at Stanford University. A past president of the Semiotic Society of America, Baron has published seven books, including *Alphabet to Email: How Written English Evolved and Where It's Heading* (2000) and *Always On: Language in an Online and Mobile World* (2008).

In this Op-Ed piece, Baron argues that when students rely on sound bites instead of full articles and books in their research, they lose the ability to analyze. Because information has become so easily accessible on the Web, she says, students no longer think they need to read sources in their entirety; a sentence or two out of context will suffice. She concludes that this practice has dire effects on students' education. How often do you read a complete text? How often do you read snippets? Is Baron right?

MUCH AS AUTOMOBILES DISCOURAGE WALKING, with undeniable consequences for our health and girth, textual snippets-on-demand threaten our need for the larger works from which they are extracted. Why read *Bowling Alone*—or even the shorter article upon which it builds—when you can lift a page that contains some keywords? In an attempt to coax students to search inside real books rather than relying exclusively on the Web for sources, many professors require references to printed works alongside URLs. Now that those "real" full-length publications are increasingly available and searchable online, the distinction between tangible and virtual is evaporating.

Admittedly, back in the days when research necessitated opening dozens of books in hopes of finding useful information, no one read each tome cover to cover. It is also fair to say that given how scattershot our searches sometimes were, we often missed what we were looking for. But that said, we also happened upon issues that proved more interesting than our original queries. Today's snippet literacy efficiently keeps us on the straight and narrow path, with little opportunity for fortuitous side trips.

Google's recent foray into massive library storage has led the publishing industry to cry foul on the grounds of copyright infringement. If users can procure just the lines of text they need, why lay out good money to buy a whole book? In response, online advocates argue that access to these extracts will fuel print sales. Moreover, short written segments (a chapter, a recipe) can be sold like songs from the iTunes store.

Although this debate is important for the law and the economy, it masks a challenge that some of us find even more troubling: Will effortless random access erode our collective respect for writing as a logical, linear process? Such respect matters because it undergirds modern education, which is premised on thought, evidence, and analysis rather than memorization and dogma. Reading successive pages and chapters teaches us how to follow a sustained line of reasoning.

If we approach the written word primarily through search-and- 5
seizure rather than sustained encounter-and-contemplation, we risk losing a critical element of what it means to be an educated, literate society.

STUDY QUESTIONS

1. According to Baron, how did students conduct RESEARCH in the past? How do they conduct research now?

2. What EVIDENCE does Baron provide to support her CLAIM about the CAUSE-AND-EFFECT relationship between students' intellectual development and what they read? How effective is her evidence? Explain.

3. *For Writing.* Consider what you read. Text messages from friends? Complete magazine articles? Online news briefs? Short stories? Novels? All of the above? Write an essay in which you agree or disagree (or both) with Baron, using evidence from your own experiences with reading to support your claim(s).

JOAN DIDION { *On Keeping a Notebook*

JOAN DIDION (b. 1934), a prolific writer whose body of work includes novels, screenplays, and book reviews, is especially well known for her keen social observation. Two of her most popular essay collections are *Slouching Towards Bethlehem* (1969) and *The White Album* (1979). The former is considered a classic of New Journalism, a style of writing that combines elements of fiction with reporting. Her recent memoir, *The Year of Magical Thinking* (2005), describes her slow, painful adjustment to the loss of her husband and the illness of her daughter. In 2007, Didion wrote a drama based on the memoir; the play ran on Broadway for twenty-four weeks.

In "On Keeping a Notebook," originally published in *Slouching Towards Bethlehem*, Didion examines her notebooks, contrasts them with diaries, and explains the purposes her notebooks serve. As she reminisces about the specific people and events she has recorded in her notebooks, she speculates about the person who, although absent, is the real subject of these entries: Didion herself. Notice how this essay is organized and consider what effect its structure has on you as a reader. If you keep a notebook, journal, or diary, think about why you do and what you are trying to record.

———

"'THAT WOMAN ESTELLE,'" THE NOTE reads, " 'is partly the reason why George Sharp and I are separated today.' *Dirty crepe-de-Chine wrapper, hotel bar, Wilmington RR, 9:45 a.m. August Monday morning.*"

Since the note is in my notebook, it presumably has some meaning to me. I study it for a long while. At first I have only the most general notion of what I was doing on an August Monday morning in the bar of the hotel across from the Pennsylvania Railroad station in Wilmington, Delaware (waiting for a train? missing one? 1960? 1961? why Wilmington?), but I do remember being there. The woman in the dirty crepe-de-Chine wrapper had come down from her room for a beer, and the bartender had heard before the reason why George Sharp and she were separated today. "Sure," he said, and went on mopping the floor. "You told me." At the other end of the bar is a girl. She is talking, pointedly, not to the man beside her but to a cat lying in the triangle of sunlight cast through the open door. She is wearing a plaid silk dress from Peck & Peck, and the hem is coming down.

Here is what it is: the girl has been on the Eastern Shore, and now she is going back to the city, leaving the man beside her, and all she can see ahead are the viscous summer sidewalks and the 3 a.m. long-distance calls that will make her lie awake and then sleep drugged through all the steaming mornings left in August (1960? 1961?). Because she must go directly from the train to lunch in New York, she wishes that she had a safety pin for the hem of the plaid silk dress, and she also wishes that she could forget about the hem and the lunch and stay in the cool bar that smells of disinfectant and malt and make friends with the woman in the crepe-de-Chine wrapper. She is afflicted by a little self-pity, and she wants to compare Estelles. That is what that was all about.

Why did I write it down? In order to remember, of course, but exactly what was it I wanted to remember? How much of it actually happened? Did any of it? Why do I keep a notebook at all? It is easy to deceive oneself on all those scores. The impulse to write things down is a peculiarly compulsive one, inexplicable to those who do not share it, useful only accidentally, only secondarily, in the way that any compulsion tries to justify itself. I suppose that it begins or does not begin in the cradle. Although I have felt compelled to write things down since I was five years old, I doubt that my daughter ever will, for she is a singularly blessed and accepting child, delighted with life exactly as life presents itself to her, unafraid to go to sleep and unafraid to wake up. Keepers of private notebooks are a different breed altogether, lonely and resistant rearrangers of things, anxious malcontents, children afflicted apparently at birth with some presentiment of loss.

My first notebook was a Big Five tablet, given to me by my mother 5 with the sensible suggestion that I stop whining and learn to amuse myself by writing down my thoughts. She returned the tablet to me a few years ago; the first entry is an account of a woman who believed herself to be freezing to death in the Arctic night, only to find, when day broke, that she had stumbled onto the Sahara Desert, where she would die of the heat before lunch. I have no idea what turn of a five-year-old's mind could have prompted so insistently "ironic" and exotic a story, but it does reveal a certain predilection for the extreme which has dogged me into adult life; perhaps if I were analytically inclined I would find it a truer story than any I might have told about Donald Johnson's birthday party or the day my cousin Brenda put Kitty Litter in the aquarium.

So the point of my keeping a notebook has never been, nor is it now, to have an accurate factual record of what I have been doing or thinking. That would be a different impulse entirely, an instinct for reality which I sometimes envy but do not possess. At no point have I ever been able successfully to keep a diary; my approach to daily life ranges from the grossly negligent to the merely absent, and on those few occasions when I have tried dutifully to record a day's events, boredom has so overcome me that the results are mysterious at best. What is this business about "shopping, typing piece, dinner with E, depressed"? Shopping for what? Typing what piece? Who is E? Was this "E" depressed, or was I depressed? Who cares?

In fact I have abandoned altogether that kind of pointless entry; instead I tell what some would call lies. "That's simply not true," the members of my family frequently tell me when they come up against my memory of a shared event. "The party was *not* for you, the spider was *not* a black widow, *it wasn't that way at all.*" Very likely they are right, for not only have I always had trouble distinguishing between what happened and what merely might have happened, but I remain unconvinced that the distinction, for my purposes, matters. The cracked crab that I recall having for lunch the day my father came home from Detroit in 1945 must certainly be embroidery, worked into the day's pattern to lend verisimilitude; I was ten years old and would not now remember the cracked crab. The day's events did not turn on cracked crab. And yet it is precisely that fictitious crab that makes me see the afternoon all over again, a home movie run all too often, the father bearing gifts, the child weeping, an exercise in family love and guilt. Or that is what it was to me. Similarly, perhaps it never did snow that August in Vermont; perhaps there never were flurries in the night wind, and maybe no one else felt the ground hardening and summer already dead even as we pretended to bask in it, but that was how it felt to me, and it might as well have snowed, could have snowed, did snow.

How it felt to me: that is getting closer to the truth about a notebook. I sometimes delude myself about why I keep a notebook, imagine that some thrifty virtue derives from preserving everything observed. See enough and write it down, I tell myself, and then some morning when the world seems drained of wonder, some day when I am only going through the motions of doing what I am supposed to do, which is write—on that bankrupt morning I will simply open my notebook and there it will all be, a forgotten account with accumulated interest, paid passage back to the world out there: dialogue overheard in hotels and elevators and at the hatcheck counter in Pavillon (one middle-aged man shows his hat check to another and says, "That's my old football number"); impressions of Bettina Aptheker and Benjamin Sonnenberg and Teddy ("Mr. Acapulco") Stauffer; careful *aperçus*[1] about tennis bums and failed fashion models and Greek shipping heiresses, one of whom taught me a significant lesson (a lesson I could have learned from F. Scott Fitzgerald, but perhaps we all must meet the very rich for ourselves) by asking, when I arrived to interview her in her orchid-filled sitting room on the second day of a paralyzing New York blizzard, whether it was snowing outside.

I imagine, in other words, that the notebook is about other people. But of course it is not. I have no real business with what one stranger said to another at the hatcheck counter in Pavillon; in fact I suspect that the line "That's my old football number" touched not my own imagination at all, but merely some memory of something once read,

[1]Observations (French).

probably "The Eighty-Yard Run."[2] Nor is my concern with a woman in a dirty crepe-de-Chine wrapper in a Wilmington bar. My stake is always, of course, in the unmentioned girl in the plaid silk dress. *Remember what it was to be me:* that is always the point.

It is a difficult point to admit. We are brought up in the ethic that oth- 10 ers, any others, all others, are by definition more interesting than our- selves; taught to be diffident, just this side of self-effacing. ("You're the least important person in the room and don't forget it," Jessica Mitford's[3] governess would hiss in her ear on the advent of any social occasion; I copied that into my notebook because it is only recently that I have been able to enter a room without hearing some such phrase in my inner ear.) Only the very young and the very old may recount their dreams at breakfast, dwell upon self, interrupt with memories of beach picnics and favorite Liberty lawn dresses and the rainbow trout in a creek near Colorado Springs. The rest of us are expected, rightly, to affect absorption in other people's favorite dresses, other people's trout.

And so we do. But our notebooks give us away, for however dutifully we record what we see around us, the common denominator of all we see is always, transparently, shamelessly, the implacable "I." We are not talking here about the kind of notebook that is patently for public con- sumption, a structural conceit for binding together a series of graceful *pensées;*[4] we are talking about something private, about bits of the mind's string too short to use, an indiscriminate and erratic assemblage with meaning only for its maker.

And sometimes even the maker has difficulty with the meaning. There does not seem to be, for example, any point in my knowing for the rest of my life that, during 1964, 720 tons of soot fell on every square mile of New York City, yet there it is in my notebook, labeled "FACT." Nor do I really need to remember that Ambrose Bierce liked to spell Leland Stanford's name "£eland $tanford"[5] or that "smart

[2]A 1955 short story by novelist Irwin Shaw.
[3]British-born writer (1917–96) best known as an investigative journalist.
[4]Thoughts (French).
[5]American businessman (1824–93) and founder of Stanford University. Ambrose Bierce (1842–1914?) was an American journalist and satirist.

women almost always wear black in Cuba," a fashion hint without much potential for practical application. And does not the relevance of these notes seem marginal at best?:

> In the basement museum of the Inyo County Courthouse in Independence, California, sign pinned to a mandarin coat: "This MAN-DARIN COAT was often worn by Mrs. Minnie S. Brooks when giving lectures on her TEAPOT COLLECTION."

> Redhead getting out of car in front of Beverly Wilshire Hotel, chinchilla stole, Vuitton bags with tags reading:

MRS LOU FOX

HOTEL SAHARA

VEGAS

Well, perhaps not entirely marginal. As a matter of fact, Mrs. Minnie S. Brooks and her MANDARIN COAT pull me back into my own childhood, for although I never knew Mrs. Brooks and did not visit Inyo County until I was thirty, I grew up in just such a world, in houses cluttered with Indian relics and bits of gold ore and ambergris and the souvenirs my Aunt Mercy Farnsworth brought back from the Orient. It is a long way from that world to Mrs. Lou Fox's world, where we all live now, and is it not just as well to remember that? Might not Mrs. Minnie S. Brooks help me to remember what I am? Might not Mrs. Lou Fox help me to remember what I am not?

But sometimes the point is harder to discern. What exactly did I have in mind when I noted down that it cost the father of someone I know $650 a month to light the place on the Hudson in which he lived before the Crash? What use was I planning to make of this line by Jimmy Hoffa:[6] "I may have my faults, but being wrong ain't one of them"? And although I think it interesting to know where the girls who travel with the Syndicate have their hair done when they find them-

---

[6]American labor leader (b. 1913) who disappeared in 1975; he is presumed to have been murdered.

selves on the West Coast, will I ever make suitable use of it? Might I not be better off just passing it on to John O'Hara?[7] What is a recipe for sauerkraut doing in my notebook? What kind of magpie keeps this notebook? *"He was born the night the Titanic went down."* That seems a nice enough line, and I even recall who said it, but is it not really a better line in life than it could ever be in fiction?

But of course that is exactly it: not that I should ever use the line, but that I should remember the woman who said it and the afternoon I heard it. We were on her terrace by the sea, and we were finishing the wine left from lunch, trying to get what sun there was, a California winter sun. The woman whose husband was born the night the *Titanic* went down wanted to rent her house, wanted to go back to her children in Paris. I remember wishing that I could afford the house, which cost $1,000 a month. "Someday you will," she said lazily. "Someday it all comes." There in the sun on her terrace it seemed easy to believe in someday, but later I had a low-grade afternoon hangover and ran over a black snake on the way to the supermarket and was flooded with inexplicable fear when I heard the checkout clerk explaining to the man ahead of me why she was finally divorcing her husband. "He left me no choice," she said over and over as she punched the register. "He has a little seven-month-old baby by her, he left me no choice." I would like to believe that my dread then was for the human condition, but of course it was for me, because I wanted a baby and did not then have one and because I wanted to own the house that cost $1,000 a month to rent and because I had a hangover.

It all comes back. Perhaps it is difficult to see the value in having one's self back in that kind of mood, but I do see it; I think we are well advised to keep on nodding terms with the people we used to be, whether we find them attractive company or not. Otherwise they run up unannounced and surprise us, come hammering on the mind's door at 4 a.m. of a bad night and demand to know who deserted them, who betrayed them, who is going to make amends. We forget all too soon the things we thought we could never forget. We forget the loves and the betrayals alike, forget what we whispered and what we

[7]American author (1905–70), highly regarded for his skillful use of realistic dialogue.

screamed, forget who we were. I have already lost touch with a couple of people I used to be; one of them, a seventeen-year-old, presents little threat, although it would be of some interest to me to know again what it feels like to sit on a river levee drinking vodka-and-orange-juice and listening to Les Paul and Mary Ford and their echoes sing "How High the Moon"[8] on the car radio. (You see I still have the scenes, but I no longer perceive myself among those present, no longer could even improvise the dialogue.) The other one, a twenty-three-year-old, bothers me more. She was always a good deal of trouble, and I suspect she will reappear when I least want to see her, skirts too long, shy to the point of aggravation, always the injured party, full of recriminations and little hurts and stories I do not want to hear again, at once saddening me and angering me with her vulnerability and ignorance, an apparition all the more insistent for being so long banished.

It is a good idea, then, to keep in touch, and I suppose that keeping in touch is what notebooks are all about. And we are all on our own when it comes to keeping those lines open to ourselves: your notebook will never help me, nor mine you. *"So what's new in the whiskey business?"* What could that possibly mean to you? To me it means a blonde in a Pucci bathing suit sitting with a couple of fat men by the pool at the Beverly Hills Hotel. Another man approaches, and they all regard one another in silence for a while. "So what's new in the whiskey business?" one of the fat men finally says by way of welcome, and the blonde stands up, arches one foot and dips it in the pool, looking all the while at the cabaña where Baby Pignatari[9] is talking on the telephone. That is all there is to that, except that several years later I saw the blonde coming out of Saks Fifth Avenue in New York with her California complexion and a voluminous mink coat. In the harsh wind that day she looked old and irrevocably tired to me, and even the skins in the mink coat were not worked the way they were doing them that year, not the way she would have wanted them done, and there is the

---

[8]Jazz standard by Nancy Hamilton and Morgan Lewis (1940), best known by the 1951 recording by singer Mary Ford and guitarist Les Paul, featuring groundbreaking use of echo and overdubbing.
[9]Francisco "Baby" Pignatari (1916–77), Italian-born Brazilian industrialist and notorious playboy.

point of the story. For a while after that I did not like to look in the mirror, and my eyes would skim the newspapers and pick out only the deaths, the cancer victims, the premature coronaries, the suicides, and I stopped riding the Lexington Avenue IRT[1] because I noticed for the first time that all the strangers I had seen for years—the man with the seeing-eye dog, the spinster who read the classified pages every day, the fat girl who always got off with me at Grand Central—looked older than they once had.

It all comes back. Even that recipe for sauerkraut: even that brings it back. I was on Fire Island when I first made that sauerkraut, and it was raining, and we drank a lot of bourbon and ate the sauerkraut and went to bed at ten, and I listened to the rain and the Atlantic and felt safe. I made the sauerkraut again last night and it did not make me feel any safer, but that is, as they say, another story.

---

[1]New York City subway line passing through Grand Central Terminal in Manhattan.

STUDY QUESTIONS

1. What are the differences, as Didion sees them, between diaries and notebooks? Why does she prefer the latter?

2. Didion concludes that notebooks are a tool to "keep in touch" with "the people we used to be, whether we find them attractive company or not." How do you "keep in touch" with earlier versions of yourself? ANALYZE the effectiveness of these methods, intentional or not, and of any tools you use (notebooks, journals, etc.).

3. *For Writing.* Although Didion notes her family members' disagreement with her presentation of details from the past, she also goes on to say, "not only have I always had trouble distinguishing between what happened and what merely might have happened, but I remain unconvinced that the distinction, for my purposes, matters." Write an essay on the nature of memory, using either personal experience or RESEARCH to argue whether you think that the distinction between what *really* happened and what *might* have happened matters. Does your STANCE change based on context; that is, does your answer change if the record of a memory is intended to be read by others or to be kept to oneself? How does the importance of the distinction change based on the GENRE in which it is presented?

FREDERICK DOUGLASS { *Learning to Read*

FREDERICK DOUGLASS (circa 1818–1895) was born a slave in Maryland to an African American mother and an unknown father whom he believed to be white. He lived with his grandmother until her death; he was then sent to Baltimore, at the age of seven, to live with Hugh and Sophia Auld, who hired him out to work. In 1838 Douglass escaped slavery by dressing as a sailor, holding another sailor's freeman papers, and taking a twenty-four-hour journey by train and boat to New York. He continued on from there to Massachusetts, where he became an acclaimed abolitionist speaker. His autobiography, *Narrative of the Life of Frederick Douglass, an American Slave*, was published in 1845.

This selection from the *Narrative* shows Douglass's creativity and perseverance as he finds ways to learn how to read and write in an environment that is hostile to his ambitions. Pay attention not only to the process that Douglass goes through but also to what he learns when he can read— education, for him, brings painful awareness. What place does reading have in your daily life? Do you read books, newspapers, information online, text messages? How has your reading education been different from that of Douglass? Do you think reading ultimately *did* liberate Douglass?

I LIVED IN MASTER HUGH'S family about seven years. During this time, I succeeded in learning to read and write. In accomplishing this, I was compelled to resort to various stratagems. I had no regular teacher. My mistress, who had kindly commenced to instruct me, had, in compliance with the advice and direction of her husband, not only ceased to instruct, but had set her face against my being instructed by any one else. It is due, however, to my mistress to say of her, that she did not adopt this course of treatment immediately. She at first lacked the depravity indispensable to shutting me up in mental darkness. It was at least necessary for her to have some training in the exercise of ir-responsible power, to make her equal to the task of treating me as though I were a brute.

My mistress was, as I have said, a kind and tender-hearted woman; and in the simplicity of her soul she commenced, when I first went to live with her, to treat me as she supposed one human being ought to treat another. In entering upon the duties of a slaveholder, she did not seem to perceive that I sustained to her the relation of a mere chattel, and that for her to treat me as a human being was not only wrong, but dangerously so. Slavery proved as injurious to her as it did to me. When I went there, she was a pious, warm, and tender-hearted woman. There was no sorrow or suffering for which she had not a tear. She had bread for the hungry, clothes for the naked, and comfort for every mourner that came within her reach. Slavery soon proved its ability to divest her of these heavenly qualities. Under its influence, the tender heart became stone, and the lamblike disposition gave way to one of tigerlike fierceness. The first step in her downward course was in her ceasing to instruct me. She now commenced to practise her husband's precepts. She finally became even more violent in her opposition than her husband himself. She was not satisfied with simply doing as well as he had commanded; she seemed anxious to do better. Nothing seemed to make her more angry than to see me with a newspaper. She seemed to think that here lay the danger. I have had her rush at me with a face made all up of fury, and snatch from me a newspaper, in a manner that fully revealed her apprehension. She was an apt woman; and a little ex-perience soon demonstrated, to her satisfaction, that education and slavery were incompatible with each other.

From this time I was most narrowly watched. If I was in a separate room any considerable length of time, I was sure to be suspected of having a book, and was at once called to give an account of myself. All this, however, was too late. The first step had been taken. Mistress, in teaching me the alphabet, had given me the *inch*, and no precaution could prevent me from taking the *ell*.[1]

The plan which I adopted, and the one by which I was most suc-

---

[1]An archaic unit of measurement equal to forty-five inches.

cessful, was that of making friends of all the little white boys whom I met in the street. As many of these as I could, I converted into teachers. With their kindly aid, obtained at different times and in different places, I finally succeeded in learning to read. When I was sent of errands, I always took my book with me, and by going one part of my errand quickly, I found time to get a lesson before my return. I used also to carry bread with me, enough of which was always in the house, and to which I was always welcome; for I was much better off in this regard than many of the poor white children in our neighborhood. This bread I used to bestow upon the hungry little urchins, who, in return, would give me that more valuable bread of knowledge. I am strongly tempted to give the names of two or three of those little boys, as a testimonial of the gratitude and affection I bear them; but prudence forbids;—not that it would injure me, but it might embarrass them; for it is almost an unpardonable offence to teach slaves to read in this Christian country. It is enough to say of the dear little fellows, that they lived on Philpot Street, very near Durgin and Bailey's shipyard. I used to talk this matter of slavery over with them. I would sometimes say to them, I wished I could be as free as they would be when they got to be men. "You will be free as soon as you are twenty-one, *but I am a slave for life!* Have not I as good a right to be free as you have?" These words used to trouble them; they would express for me the liveliest sympathy, and console me with the hope that something would occur by which I might be free.

I was now about twelve years old, and the thought of being *a slave* 5 *for life* began to bear heavily upon my heart. Just about this time, I got hold of a book entitled "The Columbian Orator."[2] Every opportunity I got, I used to read this book. Among much of other interesting matter, I found in it a dialogue between a master and his slave. The slave was represented as having run away from his master three times. The dialogue represented the conversation which took place between them, when the slave was retaken the third time. In this dialogue, the whole argument in behalf of slavery was brought forward by the master, all of which was disposed of by the slave. The slave was made to say some

[2]First published in 1797, this anthology was used to teach rhetorical skills.

very smart as well as impressive things in reply to his master—things which had the desired though unexpected effect; for the conversation resulted in the voluntary emancipation of the slave on the part of the master.

In the same book, I met with one of Sheridan's mighty speeches on and in behalf of Catholic emancipation.[3] These were choice documents to me. I read them over and over again with unabated interest. They gave tongue to interesting thoughts of my own soul, which had frequently flashed through my mind, and died away for want of utterance. The moral which I gained from the dialogue was the power of truth over the conscience of even a slaveholder. What I got from Sheridan was a bold denunciation of slavery, and a powerful vindication of human rights. The reading of these documents enabled me to utter my thoughts, and to meet the arguments brought forward to sustain slavery; but while they relieved me of one difficulty, they brought on another even more painful than the one of which I was relieved. The more I read, the more I was led to abhor and detest my enslavers. I could regard them in no other light than a band of successful robbers, who had left their homes, and gone to Africa, and stolen us from our homes, and in a strange land reduced us to slavery. I loathed them as being the meanest as well as the most wicked of men. As I read and contemplated the subject, behold! that very discontentment which Master Hugh had predicted would follow my learning to read had already come, to torment and sting my soul to unutterable anguish. As I writhed under it, I would at times feel that learning to read had been a curse rather than a blessing. It had given me a view of my wretched condition, without the remedy. It opened my eyes to the horrible pit, but to no ladder upon which to get out. In moments of agony, I envied my fellow-slaves for their stupidity. I have often wished myself a beast. I preferred the condition of the meanest reptile to my own. Any thing, no matter what, to get rid of thinking! It was this everlasting thinking of my condition that tormented me. There was no getting rid of it. It was pressed upon me by every object within sight or hearing, animate

---

[3]Richard Brinsley Sheridan (1751–1815), Irish playwright and political leader. The speech is by Arthur O'Connor, an Irish politician.

or inanimate. The silver trump of freedom had roused my soul to eternal wakefulness. Freedom now appeared, to disappear no more forever. It was heard in every sound, and seen in every thing. It was ever present to torment me with a sense of my wretched condition. I saw nothing without seeing it, I heard nothing without hearing it, and felt nothing without feeling it. It looked from every star, it smiled in every calm, breathed in every wind, and moved in every storm.

I often found myself regretting my own existence, and wishing myself dead; and but for the hope of being free, I have no doubt but that I should have killed myself, or done something for which I should have been killed. While in this state of mind, I was eager to hear any one speak of slavery. I was a ready listener. Every little while, I could hear something about the abolitionists. It was some time before I found what the word meant. It was always used in such connections as to make it an interesting word to me. If a slave ran away and succeeded in getting clear, or if a slave killed his master, set fire to a barn, or did any thing very wrong in the mind of a slaveholder, it was spoken of as the fruit of *abolition*. Hearing the word in this connection very often, I set about learning what it meant. The dictionary afforded me little or no help. I found it was "the act of abolishing"; but then I did not know what was to be abolished. Here I was perplexed. I did not dare to ask any one about its meaning, for I was satisfied that it was something they wanted me to know very little about. After a patient waiting, I got one of our city papers, containing an account of the number of petitions from the north, praying for the abolition of slavery in the District of Columbia, and of the slave trade between the States. From this time I understood the words *abolition* and *abolitionist*, and always drew near when that word was spoken, expecting to hear something of importance to myself and fellow-slaves. The light broke in upon me by degrees. I went one day down on the wharf of Mr. Waters; and seeing two Irishmen unloading a scow of stone, I went, unasked, and helped them. When we had finished, one of them came to me and asked me if I were a slave. I told him I was. He asked, "Are ye a slave for life?" I told him that I was. The good Irishman seemed to be deeply affected by the statement. He said to the other that it was a pity so fine a little fellow as myself should be a slave for life. He said it was a shame to hold me. They both advised me to run away to the north; that I should find friends there, and that I should be free. I pretended not to be interested in what they said, and treated them as if I did not understand them; for I feared they might be treacherous. White men have been known to encourage slaves to escape, and then, to get the reward, catch them and return them to their masters. I was afraid that these seemingly good men might use me so; but I nevertheless remembered their advice, and from that time I resolved to run away. I looked forward to a time at which it would be safe for me to escape. I was too young to think of doing so immediately; besides, I wished to learn how to write, as I might have occasion to write my own pass. I consoled myself with the hope that I should one day find a good chance. Meanwhile, I would learn to write.

The idea as to how I might learn to write was suggested to me by being in Durgin and Bailey's ship-yard, and frequently seeing the ship carpenters, after hewing, and getting a piece of timber ready for use, write on the timber the name of that part of the ship for which it was intended. When a piece of timber was intended for the larboard side, it would be marked thus—"L." When a piece was for the starboard side, it would be marked thus—"S." A piece for the larboard side forward, would be marked thus—"L. F." When a piece was for starboard side forward, it would be marked thus—"S. F." For larboard aft, it would be marked thus—"L. A." For starboard aft, it would be marked thus—"S. A." I soon learned the names of these letters, and for what they were intended when placed upon a piece of timber in the shipyard. I immediately commenced copying them, and in a short time was able to make the four letters named. After that, when I met with any boy who I knew could write, I would tell him I could write as well as he. The next word would be, "I don't believe you. Let me see you try it." I would then make the letters which I had been so fortunate as to learn, and ask him to beat that. In this way I got a good many lessons in writing, which it is quite possible I should never have gotten in any other way. During this time, my copy-book was the board fence, brick wall, and pavement; my pen and ink was a lump of chalk. With these, I learned mainly how to write. I then commenced and continued copying the Italics in Webster's Spelling Book,[4] until I could make them all without looking on the book. By this time, my little Master Thomas had gone to school, and learned how to write, and had written over a number of copy-books. These had been brought home, and shown to some of our near neighbors, and then laid aside. My mistress used to go to class meeting at the Wilk Street meetinghouse every Monday afternoon, and leave me to take care of the house. When left thus, I used to spend the time in writing in the spaces left in Master Thomas's copy-book, copying what he had written. I continued to do this until I could write a hand very similar to that of Master Thomas. Thus, after a long, tedious effort for years, I finally succeeded in learning how to write.

[4]*The American Spelling Book* (1783) by Noah Webster (1758–1843).

STUDY QUESTIONS

1. Why does Douglass's first teacher abandon his lessons? Why does reading become a curse, rather than a blessing, to him?

2. EXPLAIN THE PROCESS of how Douglass learns to read. Which methods seem most effective? How does Douglass CHARACTERIZE himself throughout the process? How does his CHARACTER change as he learns to read?

3. *For Writing.* Compose your own LITERACY NARRATIVE, in which you analyze the process of doing something literary—perhaps reading a challenging novel, writing an essay, teaching someone else to read. Your narrative does not have to end in triumph, but it should attempt to tease out the nuances of the situation.

PETER ELBOW { *Desperation Writing*

PETER ELBOW (b. 1935), Professor Emeritus of English at the University of Massachusetts, Amherst, revolutionized the teaching of writing with his work on pedagogy and writing theory. Drawing upon his own difficulty with writing during his undergraduate education at Williams College, Elbow has devoted his career to helping writers overcome their own inner hindrances to writing freely and effectively. One of Elbow's enduring contributions to writing classes is the practice of "freewriting," which asks the writer to put down on paper whatever he or she is thinking of, without regard to organization or coherence. Elbow has published numerous essays in periodicals such as *College English* and *A Journal of Higher Education*. His books include *Writing with Power: Techniques for Mastering the Writing Process* (1981) and *Being a Writer* (2002).

In "Desperation Writing," Elbow addresses a common anxiety for writers: how do you write something when you're facing a deadline but you're feeling incapable of coherent thought? Elbow analyzes his writing process for this situation and, in doing so, demonstrates that a writer *always* has ideas—he or she just has to locate the useful ones and then develop them into coherent units. How does your own writing process, whether driven by desperation or not, compare with the one that Elbow advocates?As you read, think about Elbow's audience and how well he reaches it.

I KNOW I AM NOT alone in my recurring twinges of panic that I won't be able to write something when I need to, I won't be able to produce coherent speech or thought. And that lingering doubt is a great hinderance to writing. It's a constant fog or static that clouds the mind. I never got out of its clutches till I discovered that it was possible to write something—not something great or pleasing but at least something usable, workable—when my mind is out of commission. The trick is that you have to do all your cooking out on the table: your mind is incapable of doing any inside. It means using symbols and pieces of paper not as a crutch but as a wheel chair.

The first thing is to admit your condition: because of some mood or event or whatever, your mind is incapable of anything that could be called thought. It can put out a babbling kind of speech utterance, it can put a simple feeling, perception, or sort-of-thought into understandable (though terrible) words. But it is incapable of considering anything in relation to anything else. The moment you try to hold that thought or feeling up against some other to see the relationship, you simply lose the picture—you get nothing but buzzing lines or waving colors.

So admit this. Avoid anything more than one feeling, perception, or thought. Simply write as much as possible. Try simply to steer your mind in the direction or general vicinity of the thing you are trying to write about and start writing and keep writing.

Just write and keep writing. (Probably best to write on only one side of the paper in case you should want to cut parts out with scissors—but you probably won't.) Just write and keep writing. It will probably come in waves. After a flurry, stop and take a brief rest. But don't stop too long. Don't think about what you are writing or what you have written or else you will overload the circuit again. Keep writing as though you are drugged or drunk. Keep doing this till you feel you have a lot of material that might be useful; or, if necessary, till you can't stand it anymore—even if you doubt that there's anything useful there.

Then take a pad of little pieces of paper—or perhaps 3 × 5 cards— 5
and simply start at the beginning of what you were writing, and as you read over what you wrote, every time you come to any thought, feeling, perception, or image that could be gathered up into one sentence or

one assertion, do so and write it by itself on a little sheet of paper. In short, you are trying to turn, say, ten or twenty pages of wandering mush into twenty or thirty hard little crab apples. Sometimes there won't be many on a page. But if it seems to you that there are none on a page, you are making a serious error—the same serious error that put you in this comatose state to start with. You are mistaking lousy, stupid, second-rate, wrong, childish, foolish, worthless ideas for no ideas at all. Your job is not to pick out *good* ideas but to pick out ideas. As long as you were conscious, your words will be full of things that could be called feelings, utterances, ideas—things that can be squeezed into one simple sentence. This is your job. Don't ask for too much.

After you have done this, take those little slips or cards, read through them a number of times—not struggling with them, simply wandering and mulling through them; perhaps shifting them around and looking through them in various sequences. In a sense these are cards you are playing solitaire with, and the rules of this particular game permit shuffling the unused pile.

The goal of this procedure with the cards is to get them to distribute themselves in two or three or ten or fifteen different piles on your desk. You can get them to do this almost by themselves if you simply keep reading through them in different orders; certain cards will begin to feel like they go with other cards. I emphasize this passive, thoughtless mode because I want to talk about desperation writing in its pure state. In practice, almost invariably at some point in the procedure, your sanity begins to return. It is often at this point. You actually are moved to have thoughts or—and the difference between active and passive is crucial here—to *exert* thought: to hold two cards together and *build* or *assert* a relationship. It is a matter of bringing energy to bear.

So you may start to be able to do something active with these cards, and begin actually to think. But if not, just allow the cards to find their own piles with each other by feel, by drift, by intuition, by mindlessness.

You have now engaged in the two main activities that will permit you to get something cooked out on the table rather than in your brain: writing out into messy words, summing up into single assertions, and even sensing relationships between assertions. You can simply continue to deploy these two activities.

If, for example, after that first round of writing, assertion-making, and pile-making, your piles feel as though they are useful and satisfactory for what you are writing—paragraphs or sections or trains of thought—then you can carry on from there. See if you can gather each pile up into a single assertion. When you can, then put the subsidiary assertions of that pile into their best order to fit with that single unifying one. If you *can't* get the pile into one assertion, then take the pile as the basis for doing some more writing out into words. In the course of this writing, you may produce for yourself the single unifying assertion you were looking for; or you may have to go through the cycle of turning the writing into assertions and piles and so forth. Perhaps more than once. The pile may turn out to want to be two or more piles itself; or it may want to become part of a pile you already have. This is natural. This kind of meshing into one configuration, then coming apart, then coming together and meshing into a different configuration—this is growing and cooking. It makes a terrible mess, but if you can't do it in your head, you have to put up with a cluttered desk and a lot of confusion.

If, on the other hand, all that writing *didn't* have useful material in it, it means that your writing wasn't loose, drifting, quirky, jerky, associative enough. This time try especially to let things simply remind you of things that are seemingly crazy or unrelated. Follow these odd associations. Make as many metaphors as you can—be as nutty as possible—and explore the metaphors themselves—open them out. You may have all your energy tied up in some area of your experience that you are leaving out. Don't refrain from writing about whatever else is on your mind: how you feel at the moment, what you are losing your mind over, randomness that intrudes itself on your consciousness, the pattern on the wallpaper, what those people you see out the window have on their minds—though keep coming back to the whateveritis you are supposed to be writing about. Treat it, in short, like ten-minute writing exercises. Your best perceptions and thoughts are always going to be tied up in whatever is really occupying you, and that is also where your energy is. You may end up writing a love poem—or a hate poem—in one of those little piles while the other piles will finally turn into a lab report on data processing or whatever you have to write about. But you couldn't, in your present state of having your head shot off, have written that report without also writing the poem. And the report will have some of the juice of the poem in it and vice versa.

STUDY QUESTIONS

1. What steps does Elbow recommend taking when you are writing in "desperation"?

2. In this ANALYSIS of the writing PROCESS, how does Elbow conceive of the relationship between thoughts and the ideas on the page? How does he use this process to move beyond a writer's panic?

3. Who do you think is Elbow's AUDIENCE? How and how well does he appeal to that audience? Refer to passages from the essay in your RESPONSE.

4. *For Writing.* Choose a TOPIC and follow Elbow's process to GENERATE IDEAS and eventually write a cohesive two-to-three-page essay. Then, in an essay, evaluate how well this process worked for you. What worked well? What did not? How well does this process work if you are not feeling "desperate"? What part(s) of Elbow's process can you to apply to any writing situation? Do you think you'll use this process in the future? Why or why not?

STANLEY FISH   { *Devoid of Content*

STANLEY FISH (b. 1938), American literary critic and legal scholar, was
born and raised in Providence, Rhode Island. After receiving his PhD in
English from Yale University in 1962, Fish went on to teach at the
University of California, Berkeley, Johns Hopkins University, and
Duke University. In 1999 he became the Dean of Liberal Arts and Sciences
at the University of Illinois, Chicago, and in 2005 he became a professor of
humanities and law at Florida International University. Fish has authored
ten books and he frequently contributes opinion pieces to the *New York
Times*, where the following essay first appeared.

In "Devoid of Content," Fish asks why every year millions of students
graduate from American high schools and colleges unable to write coherent
English sentences. The answer, he finds, is that writing is taught with an
emphasis on content rather than form. Instead of having students write
about ideas, Fish argues, the way to teach students to write is to teach them
the structure of language: grammar and syntax. As you read his argument,
consider the process by which Fish teaches grammar and syntax in his own
writing classes, and think about how his explanation of that process works
to support his claim.

———————————

WE ARE AT THAT TIME of year when millions of American college and
high school students will stride across the stage, take diploma in hand
and set out to the wider world, most of them utterly unable to write a
clear and coherent English sentence. How is this possible? The

answer is simple and even obvious: Students can't write clean English sentences because they are not being taught what sentences are.

Most composition courses that American students take today emphasize content rather than form, on the theory that if you chew over big ideas long enough, the ability to write about them will (mysteriously) follow. The theory is wrong. Content is a lure and a delusion, and it should be banished from the classroom. Form is the way.

On the first day of my freshman writing class I give the students this assignment: You will be divided into groups and by the end of the semester each group will be expected to have created its own language, complete with a syntax, a lexicon, a text, rules for translating the text and strategies for teaching your language to fellow students. The language you create cannot be English or a slightly coded version of English, but it must be capable of indicating the distinctions—between tense, number, manner, mood, agency and the like—that English enables us to make.

You can imagine the reaction of students who think that "syntax" is something cigarette smokers pay, guess that "lexicon" is the name of a rebel tribe inhabiting a galaxy far away, and haven't the slightest idea of what words like "tense," "manner" and "mood" mean. They think I'm crazy. Yet 14 weeks later—and this happens every time—each group has produced a language of incredible sophistication and precision.

How is this near miracle accomplished? The short answer is that over the semester the students come to understand a single proposition: A sentence is a structure of logical relationships. In its bare form, this proposition is hardly edifying, which is why I immediately supplement it with a simple exercise. "Here," I say, "are five words randomly chosen; turn them into a sentence." (The first time I did this the words were coffee, should, book, garbage and quickly.) In no time at all I am presented with 20 sentences, all perfectly coherent and all quite different. Then comes the hard part. "What is it," I ask, "that you did? What did it take to turn a random list of words into a sentence?" A lot of fumbling and stumbling and false starts follow, but finally someone says, "I put the words into a relationship with one another."

51

Once the notion of relationship is on the table, the next question almost asks itself: what exactly are the relationships? And working with the sentences they have created the students quickly realize two things: first, that the possible relationships form a limited set; and second, that it all comes down to an interaction of some kind between actors, the actions they perform and the objects of those actions.

The next step (and this one takes weeks) is to explore the devices by which English indicates and distinguishes between the various components of these interactions. If in every sentence someone is doing something to someone or something else, how does English allow you to tell who is the doer and whom (or what) is the doee; and how do you know whether there is one doer or many; and what tells you that the doer is doing what he or she does in this way and at this time rather than another?

Notice that these are not questions about how a particular sentence works, but questions about how any sentence works, and the answers will point to something very general and abstract. They will point, in fact, to the forms that, while they are themselves without content, are necessary to the conveying of any content whatsoever, at least in English.

Once the students tumble to this point, they are more than halfway to understanding the semester-long task: they can now construct a language whose forms do the same work English does, but do it differently.

In English, for example, most plurals are formed by adding an "s" 10 to nouns. Is that the only way to indicate the difference between singular and plural? Obviously not. But the language you create, I tell them, must have some regular and abstract way of conveying that distinction; and so it is with all the other distinctions—between time, manner, spatial relationships, relationships of hierarchy and subordination, relationships of equivalence and difference—languages permit you to signal.

In the languages my students devise, the requisite distinctions are signaled by any number of formal devices—word order, word endings, prefixes, suffixes, numbers, brackets, fonts, colors, you name it. Exactly how they do it is not the point; the point is that they know what it is they are trying to do; the moment they know that, they have succeeded, even if much of the detailed work remains to be done.

At this stage last semester, the representative of one group asked me, "Is it all right if we use the same root form for adjectives and adverbs, but distinguish between them by their order in the sentence?" I could barely disguise my elation. If they could formulate a question like that one, they had already learned the lesson I was trying to teach them.

In the course of learning that lesson, the students will naturally and effortlessly conform to the restriction I announce on the first day: "We don't do content in this class. By that I mean we are not interested in ideas—yours, mine or anyone else's. We don't have an anthology of readings. We don't discuss current events. We don't exchange views on hot-button issues. We don't tell each other what we think about anything—except about how prepositions or participles or relative pronouns function." The reason we don't do any of these things is that once ideas or themes are allowed in, the focus is shifted from the forms that make the organization of content possible to this or that piece of content, usually some recycled set of pros and cons about abortion, assisted suicide, affirmative action, welfare reform, the death penalty, free speech and so forth. At that moment, the task of understanding and mastering linguistic forms will have been replaced by the dubious pleasure of reproducing the well-worn and terminally dull arguments one hears or sees on every radio and TV talk show.

Students who take so-called courses in writing where such topics are the staples of discussion may believe, as their instructors surely do, that they are learning how to marshal arguments in ways that will improve their compositional skills. In fact, they will be learning nothing they couldn't have learned better by sitting around in a dorm room or a coffee shop. They will certainly not be learning anything about how language works; and without a knowledge of how language works they will be unable either to spot the formal breakdown of someone else's language or to prevent the formal breakdown of their own.

In my classes, the temptation of content is felt only fleetingly; for as 15 soon as students bend to the task of understanding the structure of language—a task with a content deeper than any they have been asked to forgo—they become completely absorbed in it and spontaneously enact the discipline I have imposed. And when there is the occasional and inevitable lapse, and some student voices his or her "opinion" about something, I don't have to do anything; for immediately some other student will turn and say, "No, that's content." When that happens, I experience pure pedagogical bliss.

STUDY QUESTIONS

1. What fault does Fish find in writing classes that focus on content? Do you agree that it is better to focus on form? Why or why not? Are there other ways to teach writing? Explain.

2. Fish is writing for a general AUDIENCE of readers. How might his essay be different if it were written for an audience of writing teachers and writing program administrators? For an audience of writing students? For an audience of parents?

3. *For Writing.* Write a LITERACY NARRATIVE about your own experiences in writing classes, whether in college, high school, or earlier. In your narrative, make a PROPOSAL for how writing classes should be taught, based on your experiences. Be sure to consider other POSITIONS and explain why you don't support them.

NATALIE GOLDBERG { *Be Specific*

NATALIE GOLDBERG (b. 1948), a poet and Zen practitioner for more than thirty years, teaches writing from a spiritual perspective. Her books about writing include *Writing Down the Bones: Freeing the Writer Within* (1986) and *Wild Mind: Living the Writer's Life* (1990). Her autobiography, *Long Quiet Highway: Waking Up in America* (1993), explores her life as both a student of Zen and a teacher of writing.

   In this compact, specific essay, Goldberg demonstrates what she is trying to teach her reader. Note how her examples highlight an object's or an individual's character. Consider how many times you use generic descriptions during an average day, and think about where and when you might be more specific.

――――――――――

BE SPECIFIC. DON'T SAY "FRUIT." Tell what kind of fruit—"It is a pomegranate." Give things the dignity of their names. Just as with human beings, it is rude to say, "Hey, girl, get in line." That "girl" has a name. (As a matter of fact, if she's at least twenty years old, she's a woman, not a "girl" at all.) Things, too, have names. It is much better to say "the geranium in the window" than "the flower in the window." "Geranium"—that one word gives us a much more specific picture. It penetrates more deeply into the beingness of that flower. It immediately gives us the scene by the window—red petals, green circular leaves, all straining toward sunlight.

   About ten years ago I decided I had to learn the names of plants and flowers in my environment. I bought a book on them and walked down the tree-lined streets of Boulder, examining leaf, bark, and seed, trying to match them up with their descriptions and names in the book. Maple, elm, oak, locust. I usually tried to cheat by asking people working in their yards the names of the flowers and trees growing there. I was amazed how few people had any idea of the names of the live beings inhabiting their little plot of land.

When we know the name of something, it brings us closer to the ground. It takes the blur out of our mind; it connects us to the earth. If I walk down the street and see "dogwood," "forsythia," I feel more friendly toward the environment. I am noticing what is around me and can name it. It makes me more awake.

If you read the poems of William Carlos Williams, you will see how specific he is about plants, trees, flowers—chicory, daisy, locust, poplar, quince, primrose, black-eyed Susan, lilacs—each has its own integrity. Williams says, "Write what's in front of your nose." It's good for us to know what is in front of our nose. Not just "daisy," but how the flower is in the season we are looking at it—"The dayseye hugging the earth/in August . . . brownedged,/green and pointed scales/armor his yellow."[1] Continue to hone your awareness: to the name, to the month, to the day, and finally to the moment.

Williams also says: "No idea, but in things." Study what is "in front 5 of your nose." By saying "geranium" instead of "flower," you are penetrating more deeply into the present and being there. The closer we can get to what's in front of our nose, the more it can teach us everything. "To see the World in a Grain of Sand, and a heaven in a Wild Flower . . ."[2]

In writing groups and classes too, it is good to quickly learn the names of all the other group members. It helps to ground you in the group and make you more attentive to each other's work.

Learn the names of everything: birds, cheese, tractors, cars, buildings. A writer is all at once everything—an architect, French cook, farmer—and at the same time, a writer is none of these things.

[1] From "Daisy" (1921) by William Carlos Williams (1883–1963).
[2] From "Auguries of Innocence" (ca. 1807) by British poet William Blake (1757–1827). The poem actually reads "To see a World in a Grain of Sand . . ."

STUDY QUESTIONS

1. Why does Goldberg encourage writers to be more specific? How useful do you find her advice? Explain.

2. What specific area of DESCRIPTION does Goldberg choose to advance her advice to be specific? Why do you think she limits her example in this way? What effect does it have on her PURPOSE?

3. *For Writing.* Keep a journal of all the things you see and encounter in a single day—buildings, classrooms, people, plants, and so forth. Take note of the colors and shapes of the buildings, their names, the layout of your classrooms, what people are wearing, how they are acting, what plants are on the grounds, and so on. Then write an essay in which you REFLECT on the effects of being so specific in your observations for that day. How did it affect your interactions with those buildings, people, and plants?

EDWARD HOAGLAND { *The Football Game in My Head*

EDWARD HOAGLAND (b. 1932), a native of New York City, earned his BA
from Harvard University in 1954. He published his first novel, *Cat Man,*
just a year later in 1955; it draws on his experiences working for a circus for
two summers during college. Now best known for his nonfiction writing
about nature and travel, particularly his journeys in Africa, Hoagland has
received many awards, including two Guggenheim fellowships (1964,
1975). He has also taught at a number of institutions, including the New
School in New York City, Beloit College, Brown University, and, before
retiring from teaching in 2005, Bennington College.

The reading included here is a personal essay about Hoagland's lifelong
stuttering. Carefully describing the physiological, psychological, and social
aspects of stuttering, Hoagland redefines stuttering not as a handicap but
instead a motivator. As you read, think about the analogies and metaphors
Hoagland uses to describe his stuttering—the football game in his head, for
instance—and how effectively they convey the experience of stuttering.

STUTTERING IS LIKE TRYING TO run with loops of rope around your
feet. And yet you feel that you *do* want to run because you may get more
words out that way before you trip: an impulse you resist so other people won't tell you to "calm down" and "relax." Because they themselves
may stammer a little bit when jittery or embarrassed, it's hard for a real
stutterer like me to convince a new acquaintance that we aren't perpet-
ually in such a nervous state and that it's quite normal for us to be at the
mercy of strangers. Strangers are usually civilized, once the rough and

sometimes inadvertently hurtful process of recognizing what is wrong with us is over (that we're not laughing, hiccuping, coughing, or whatever) and in a way we plumb them for traces of *Schadenfreude.*[1] A stutterer knows who the good guys are in any crowded room, as well as the location of each mocking gleam, and even the St. Francis[2] type, who will wait until he thinks nobody is looking to wipe a fleck of spittle off his face.

I've stuttered for more than sixty years, and the mysteries of the encumbrance still catch me up: being reminded every morning that it's engrained in my fiber, although I had forgotten in my dreams. Life can become a matter of measuring the importance of anything you have to say. Is it better to remain a pleasant cipher who ventures nothing in particular but chuckles immoderately at everyone else's conversation, or instead to subject your several companions to the ordeal of watching you struggle to expel opinions that are either blurred and vitiated, or made to sound too emphatic, by all the huffing and puffing, the facial contortions, tongue biting, blushing, and suffering? "Write it down," people often said to me in school; indeed I sold my first novel before I left college.

Self-confidence can reduce a stutter's dimensions (in that sense you do "outgrow" it), as will affection (received or felt), anger, sexual arousal, and various other hormonal or pheromonal states you may dip into in the shorter term. Yet it still lurks underfoot, like a trapdoor. I was determined not to be impeded and managed to serve a regular stint in the Army by telling the draft-board psychiatrist that I wanted to and was only stammering from "nervousness" with him. Later I also contrived to become a college professor, thanks to the patience of my early students. Nevertheless, through childhood and adolescence, when I was almost mute in public, I could talk without much difficulty to one or two close friends, and then to the particular girl I was necking with. In that case, an overlapping trust was then the lubricant, but if it began to evaporate as our hopes for permanence didn't pan out, I'd

[1]Pleasure derived from the troubles of others (German).

[2]Giovanni Francesco Bernardone (c. 1181–1226), patron saint of animals and the environment, as well as founder of the Franciscans, the Order of Friars Minor. St. Francis is often invoked, as here, as the personification of kindness.

start regretfully, apologetically but willy-nilly, to stutter with her again. Adrenaline, when I got mad, operated in a similar fashion, though only momentarily. That is, if somebody made fun of me or treated me cavalierly and a certain threshold was crossed, a spurt of chemistry would suddenly free my mouth and—like Popeye[3] grabbing a can of spinach—I could answer him. Poor Billy Budd[4] didn't learn this technique (and his example frightened me because of its larger implications). Yet many stutterers develop a snappish temperament, and from not just sheer frustration but the fact that being more than ready to "lose one's temper" (as Billy wasn't) actually helps. As in jujitsu, you can trap an opponent by employing his strength and cruelty against him; and bad guys aren't generally smart enough to know that if they wait me out, I'll bog down helplessly all over again.

Overall, however, stuttering is not so predictable. Whether rested or exhausted, fibbing or speaking the Simon-pure truth, and when in the company of chums or people whom I don't respect, I can be fluent or tied in knots. I learned young to be an attentive listener, both because my empathy for others' worries was honed by my handicap and because it was in my best interest that they talk a lot. And yet a core in you will hemorrhage if you become a mere assenter. How many opinions can you keep to yourself before you choke on them (and turn into a stick of furniture for everybody else)? So, instead, you measure what's worth specifying. If you agree with two thirds of what's being suggested, is it worth the labor of breathlessly elaborating upon the one third where you differ? There were plenty of times when a subject might come up that I knew more about than the rest of the group, and it used to gall me if I had held my peace till maybe closeted afterward with a close friend. A stymieing bashfulness can also slide a stutterer into slack language because accurate words are so much harder to say than bland ones. You're tempted to be content with an approximation

---

[3]Cartoon hero of comic strip and animations, created in 1929 by Elzie Crisler Segar. Popeye the Sailor gained his remarkable strength by eating spinach.

[4]Title character of *Billy Budd*, a novella by American author Herman Melville (1819–91). At a climactic moment in the story, Billy, a sailor on a ship, finds himself accused of mutiny, and, unable to respond because of his speech impediment, he strikes and kills his accuser, for which he is later hanged.

of what you mean in order to escape the scourge of being exact. A sort of football game is going on in your head—the tacklers live there too—and the very effort of pausing to figure out the right way to describe something will alert them to how to pull you down. Being glib and sloppy generates less blockage.

But it's important not to err in the opposite direction, on the side of tendentiousness, and insist on equal time only because you are a pain in the neck with a problem. You can stutter till your tongue bleeds and your chest is sore from heaving, but so what, if you haven't anything to say that's worth the humiliation? Better to function as a kind of tuning fork, vibrating to other people's anguish or apprehensiveness, as well as your own. A handicap can be cleansing. My scariest moments as a stutterer have been (1) when my daughter was learning to talk and briefly got the impression that she was supposed to do the same; (2) once when I was in the woods and a man shot in my direction and I had to make myself heard loud and fast; and (3) when anticipating weddings where I would need either to propose a toast or say "I do." Otherwise my impediment ceased to be a serious blight about the time I lost my virginity: just a sort of cleft to step around—a squint and gasp of hesitation that indicated to people I might want to be friends with or interview that I wasn't perfect either and perhaps they could trust me.

At worst, during my teens, when I was stuttering on vowels as well as consonants and spitting a few words out could seem interminable, I tried some therapies. But "Slow Speech" was as slow as the trouble itself; and repeatedly writing the first letter of the word that I was stuttering on with my finger in my pocket looked peculiar enough to attract almost as much attention. It did gradually lighten with my maturity and fatherhood, professional recognition, and the other milestones that traditionally help. Nothing "slew" it, though, until at nearly sixty I went semiblind for a couple of years, and this emergency eclipsed—completely trumped—the lesser difficulty. I felt I simply had to talk or die, and so I talked. Couldn't do it gratuitously or lots, but I talked enough to survive. The stutter somehow didn't hold water and ebbed away, until surgery restored my vision and then it returned, like other normalcies.

Such variations can make a stutter seem like a sort of ancillary eccentricity, or a personal Godzilla. But the ball carrier in your head is going to have his good days too— when he can swivel past the tacklers, improvising a broken-field dash so that they are out of position—or even capture their attention with an idea so intriguing that they stop and listen. Not for long, however: The message underlying a stutter is rather like mortality, after all. Real reprieves and fluency are not for you and me. We blunder along, stammering—then not so much—through minor scrapes and scares, but not unscathed. We're not Demosthenes,[5] of course. And poor Demosthenes, if you look him up, ended about as sadly as Billy Budd. People tend to.

[5]Ancient Greek statesman (384–22 BCE.), often cited, as here, as a superb orator. He died by taking poison rather than face capture by his enemies; his final words are remembered for their grace and eloquence.

STUDY QUESTIONS

1. How does Hoagland characterize stuttering? How does he see it as an advantage as well as an impediment? When does he not stutter?

2. How would you characterize Hoagland's ETHOS in this essay? Support your response with specific passages from the text. How does his ethos affect your reaction to his essay as a reader? How effective is it?

3. *For Writing.* Research the phenomenon of so-called phatic verbal tics—conversational filler words such as "like," "kind of," and "you know." Choose two of them, and write an essay in which you ANALYZE their function in everyday speech. What effect do they have on conversation? Why do we use them?

GARRISON KEILLOR { *How to Write a Letter*

GARRISON KEILLOR (b. 1942), well known for his public radio programs, began his career at a college radio station. He was hired by Minnesota Public Radio in 1969 and in 1974 created his weekly show, *A Prairie Home Companion*, featuring a mythical Minnesota town, Lake Wobegon. The program has run for more than thirty years and spawned several books by Keillor, as well as earning him a place in the Radio Hall of Fame.

In this process analysis essay, Keillor celebrates the value of letter writing in an era when people can simply pick up a phone to get in touch with someone. Letters, says Keillor, are a gift, and with his trademark humor he gives detailed instructions to help us express ourselves to those we love.

WE SHY PERSONS NEED TO write a letter now and then, or else we'll dry up and blow away. It's true. And I speak as one who loves to reach for the phone, dial the number, and talk. I say, "Big Bopper[1] here— what's shakin', babes?" The telephone is to shyness what Hawaii is to February, it's a way out of the woods, *and yet:* a letter is better.

Such a sweet gift—a piece of handmade writing, in an envelope that is not a bill, sitting in our friend's path when she trudges home from a long day spent among wahoos and savages, a day our words will help repair. They don't need to be immortal, just sincere. She can read them twice and again tomorrow: *You're someone I care about, Corinne, and think of often and every time I do you make me smile.*

[1]Early rock and roll star Jiles Perry "J. P." Richardson (1930–59), who used a telephone as a prop when he sang his best-known song, "Chantilly Lace."

We need to write, otherwise nobody will know who we are. They will have only a vague impression of us as A Nice Person, because, frankly, we don't shine at conversation, we lack the confidence to thrust our faces forward and say, "Hi, I'm Heather Hooten; let me tell you about my week." Mostly we say "Uh-huh" and "Oh, really." People smile and look over our shoulder, looking for someone else to meet.

So a shy person sits down and writes a letter. To be known by another person—to meet and talk freely on the page—to be close despite distance. To escape from anonymity and be our own sweet selves and express the music of our souls.

Same thing that moves a giant rock star to sing his heart out in front 5 of 123,000 people moves us to take ballpoint in hand and write a few lines to our dear Aunt Eleanor. *We want to be known.* We want her to know that we have fallen in love, that we quit our job, that we're moving to New York, and we want to say a few things that might not get said in casual conversation: *Thank you for what you've meant to me, I am very happy right now.*

The first step in writing letters is to get over the guilt of *not* writing. You don't "owe" anybody a letter. Letters are a gift. The burning shame you feel when you see unanswered mail makes it harder to pick up a pen and makes for a cheerless letter when you finally do. *I feel bad about not writing, but I've been so busy,* etc. Skip this. Few letters are obligatory, and they are *Thanks for the wonderful gift* and *I am terribly sorry to hear about George's death* and *Yes, you're welcome to stay with us next month,* and not many more than that. Write those promptly if you want to keep your friends. Don't worry about the others, except love letters, of course. When your true love writes, *Dear Light of My Life, Joy of My Heart, O Lovely Pulsating Core of My Sensate Life,* some response is called for.

Some of the best letters are tossed off in a burst of inspiration, so keep your writing stuff in one place where you can sit down for a few minutes and (*Dear Roy, I am in the middle of a book entitled* We Are Still Married *but thought I'd drop you a line. Hi to your sweetie, too*) dash off a note to a pal. Envelopes, stamps, address book, everything in a drawer so you can write fast when the pen is hot.

A blank white eight-by-eleven sheet can look as big as Montana if the pen's not so hot—try a smaller page and write boldly. Or use a note card with a piece of fine art on the front; if your letter ain't good, at least they get the Matisse. Get a pen that makes a sensuous line, get a comfortable typewriter, a friendly word processor—whichever feels easy to the hand.

Sit for a few minutes with the blank sheet in front of you, and meditate on the person you will write to, let your friend come to mind until you can almost see her or him in the room with you. Remember the last time you saw each other and how your friend looked and what you said and what perhaps was unsaid between you, and when your friend becomes real to you, start to write.

Write the salutation—*Dear* You—and take a deep breath and plunge 10 in. A simple declarative sentence will do, followed by another and another and another. Tell us what you're doing and tell it like you were talking to us. Don't think about grammar, don't think about lit'ry style, don't try to write dramatically, just give us your news. Where did you go, who did you see, what did they say, what do you think?

If you don't know where to begin, start with the present moment: *I'm sitting at the kitchen table on a rainy Saturday morning. Everyone is gone and the house is quiet.* Let your simple description of the present moment lead to something else, let the letter drift gently along.

The toughest letter to crank out is one that is meant to impress, as we all know from writing job applications; if it's hard work to slip off a letter to a friend, maybe you're trying too hard to be terrific. A letter is only a report to someone who already likes you for reasons other than your brilliance. Take it easy.

Don't worry about form. It's not a term paper. when you come to the end of one episode, just start a new paragraph. You can go from a few lines about the sad state of pro football to the fight with your mother to your fond memories of Mexico to your cat's urinary-tract infection to a few thoughts on personal indebtedness and on to the kitchen sink and what's in it. The more you write, the easier it gets, and when you have a True True Friend to write to, a *compadre*,[2] a soul sibling, then

[2]Friend (Spanish).

it's like driving a car down a country road, you just get behind the keyboard and press on the gas.

Don't tear up the page and start over when you write a bad line—try to write your way out of it. Make mistakes and plunge on. Let the letter cook along and let yourself be bold. Outrage, confusion, love—whatever is in your mind, let it find a way to the page. Writing is a means of discovery, always, and when you come to the end and write *Yours ever* or *Hugs and kisses,* you'll know something you didn't when you wrote *Dear Pal.*

Probably your friend will put your letter away, and it'll be read again 15 a few years from now—and it will improve with age. And forty years from now, your friend's grandkids will dig it out of the attic and read it, a sweet and precious relic of the ancient eighties that gives them a sudden clear glimpse of you and her and the world we old-timers knew. You will then have created an object of art. Your simple lines about where you went, who you saw, what they said, will speak to those children and they will feel in their hearts the humanity of our times.

You can't pick up a phone and call the future and tell them about our times. You have to pick up a piece of paper.

STUDY QUESTIONS

1. List the steps for writing a letter in a short "bullet" format. List three REASONS Keillor says people should write letters. Who do you think is this essay's intended AUDIENCE? Explain.

2. Even though Keillor writes a PROCESS essay, he uses ARGUMENT to develop it. Explain how these two forms of development combine to make a forceful and effective essay—or, if you do not find it effective, explain why the combination does not work and what might work better.

3. Explain why Keillor says that writing is easier than speaking for a shy person. Is it meant to PERSUADE us to write letters, or is he simply being informative? How do you know?

4. *For Writing.* Select a person with whom you are close and write him or her a letter, following Keillor's instructions. Approach this as an actual letter rather than as an assignment.

JONATHAN KOZOL { *The Human Cost of an Illiterate Society*

JONATHAN KOZOL (b. 1936) was raised in Newton, Massachusetts, and educated at Harvard University, where he earned a degree in English literature, and at Oxford University, which he attended on a Rhodes scholarship. In 1964, inspired by the civil rights campaigns taking place around the country, Kozol began teaching elementary school in Roxbury, a low-income Boston neighborhood. His experiences as a teacher there became the basis for his first book, *Death at an Early Age: The Destruction of the Hearts and Minds of Negro Children in the Boston Public Schools* (1967). He has written more than a dozen books since then, many of them best sellers, focusing on inequalities in American society and strongly advocating for change. His best-known books include *Rachel and Her Children: Homeless Families in America* (1988), *Savage Inequalities: Children in America's Schools* (1991), and *Amazing Grace: The Lives of Children and the Conscience of a Nation* (1995).

In this chapter from his eighth book, *Illiterate America* (1985), Kozol highlights the problems that face illiterate adults, whose lack of reading skills affects every aspect of their lives and creates what Kozol calls a "circumscribed existence." Illiteracy denies adults the ability to make their own choices, says Kozol, as well as the ability to protect themselves and their families, to live frugally, even to trust others. As you read, notice the many examples Kozol uses to illustrate the effects of illiteracy and give power to his argument.

PRECAUTIONS. READ BEFORE USING.

Poison: Contains sodium hydroxide (caustic soda-lye).
Corrosive: Causes severe eye and skin damage, may cause
blindness.
Harmful or fatal if swallowed.
If swallowed, give large quantities of milk or water.
Do not induce vomiting.
Important: Keep water out of can at all times to prevent con-
tents from violently erupting . . .

—warning on a can of Drano

WE ARE SPEAKING HERE NO longer of the dangers faced by passengers on Eastern Airlines or the dollar costs incurred by U.S. corporations and taxpayers. We are speaking now of human suffering and of the ethical dilemmas that are faced by a society that looks upon such suffering with qualified concern but does not take those actions which its wealth and ingenuity would seemingly demand.

Questions of literacy, in Socrates' belief, must at length be judged as matters of morality. Socrates could not have had in mind the moral compromise peculiar to a nation like our own. Some of our Founding Fathers did, however, have this question in their minds. One of the wisest of those Founding Fathers (one who may not have been most compassionate but surely was more prescient than some of his peers) recognized the special dangers that illiteracy would pose to basic equity in the political construction that he helped to shape.

"A people who mean to be their own governors," James Madison[1] wrote, "must arm themselves with the power knowledge gives. A popular government without popular information or the means of acquiring it, is but a prologue to a farce or a tragedy, or perhaps both."

Tragedy looms larger than farce in the United States today. Illiterate citizens seldom vote. Those who do are forced to cast a vote of questionable worth. They cannot make informed decisions based on serious print information. Sometimes they can be alerted to their interests by aggressive voter education. More frequently, they vote for a face, a smile, or a style, not for a mind or character or body of beliefs.

[1]Fourth president of the United States (1751–1836); chief author of the U.S. Constitution and writer of more than one-third of the Federalist Papers.

The number of illiterate adults exceeds by 16 million the entire vote 5
cast for the winner in the 1980 presidential contest. If even one third
of all illiterates could vote, and read enough and do sufficient math to
vote in their self-interest, Ronald Reagan would not likely have been
chosen president. There is, of course, no way to know for sure. We do
know this: Democracy is a mendacious term when used by those who
are prepared to countenance the forced exclusion of one third of our
electorate. So long as 60 million people are denied significant partici-
pation, the government is neither of, nor for, nor by, the people. It is a
government, at best, of those two thirds whose wealth, skin color, or
parental privilege allows them opportunity to profit from the provoca-
tion and instruction of the written word.

The undermining of democracy in the United States is one
"expense" that sensitive Americans can easily deplore because it represents a contradiction that endangers citizens of all political positions.
The human price is not so obvious at first.

Since I first immersed myself within this work I have often had the
following dream: I find that I am in a railroad station or a large department store within a city that is utterly unknown to me and where I cannot understand the printed words. None of the signs or symbols is
familiar. Everything looks strange: like mirror writing of some kind.
Gradually I understand that I am in the Soviet Union. All the letters on
the walls around me are Cyrillic.[2] I look for my pocket dictionary but
I find that it has been mislaid. Where have I left it? Then I recall that I
forgot to bring it with me when I packed my bags in Boston. I struggle
to remember the name of my hotel. I try to ask somebody for directions. One person stops and looks at me in a peculiar way. I lose the
nerve to ask. At last I reach into my wallet for an ID card. The card is
missing. Have I lost it? Then I remember that my card was confiscated
for some reason, many years before. Around this point, I wake up in
a panic.

This panic is not so different from the misery that millions of adult
illiterates experience each day within the course of their routine existence in the U.S.A.

---

[2]The alphabet used for writing Russian and some other Slavic languages.

Illiterates cannot read the menu in a restaurant.

They cannot read the cost of items on the menu in the *window* of the   10
restaurant before they enter.

Illiterates cannot read the letters that their children bring home from their teachers. They cannot study school department circulars that tell them of the courses that their children must be taking if they hope to pass the SAT exams. They cannot help with homework. They cannot write a letter to the teacher. They are afraid to visit in the classroom. They do not want to humiliate their child or themselves.

Illiterates cannot read instructions on a bottle of prescription medicine. They cannot find out when a medicine is past the year of safe consumption; nor can they read of allergenic risks, warnings to diabetics, or the potential sedative effect of certain kinds of nonprescription pills. They cannot observe preventive health care admonitions. They cannot read about "the seven warning signs of cancer" or the indications of blood-sugar fluctuations or the risks of eating certain foods that aggravate the likelihood of cardiac arrest.

Illiterates live, in more than literal ways, an uninsured existence. They cannot understand the written details on a health insurance form. They cannot read the waivers that they sign preceding surgical procedures. Several women I have known in Boston have entered a slum hospital with the intention of obtaining a tubal ligation and have emerged a few days later after having been subjected to a hysterectomy. Unaware of their rights, incognizant of jargon, intimidated by the unfamiliar air of fear and atmosphere of ether that so many of us find oppressive in the confines even of the most attractive and expensive medical facilities, they have signed their names to documents they could not read and which nobody, in the hectic situation that prevails so often in those overcrowded hospitals that serve the urban poor, had even bothered to explain.

Childbirth might seem to be the last inalienable right of any female citizen within a civilized society. Illiterate mothers, as we shall see, already have been cheated of the power to protect their progeny against the likelihood of demolition in deficient public schools and, as a result, against the verbal servitude within which they themselves exist. Surgical denial of the right to bear that child in the first place represents an ultimate denial, an unspeakable metaphor, a final darkness that denies even the twilight gleamings of our own humanity. What greater violation of our biological, our biblical, our spiritual humanity could possibly exist than that which takes place nightly, perhaps hourly these days, within such overburdened and benighted institutions as the Boston City Hospital? Illiteracy has many costs; few are so irreversible as this.

Even the roof above one's head, the gas or other fuel for heating that 15 protects the residents of northern city slums against the threat of illness in the winter months become uncertain guarantees. Illiterates cannot read the lease that they must sign to live in an apartment which, too often, they cannot afford. They cannot manage check accounts and therefore seldom pay for anything by mail. Hours and entire days of difficult travel (and the cost of bus or other public transit) must be added to the real cost of whatever they consume. Loss of interest on the check accounts they do not have, and could not manage if they did, must be regarded as another of the excess costs paid by the citizen who is excluded from the common instruments of commerce in a numerate society.

"I couldn't understand the bills," a woman in Washington, D.C., reports, "and then I couldn't write the checks to pay them. We signed things we didn't know what they were."

Illiterates cannot read the notices that they receive from welfare offices or from the IRS. They must depend on word-of-mouth instruction from the welfare worker—or from other persons whom they have good reason to mistrust. They do not know what rights they have, what deadlines and requirements they face, what options they might choose to exercise. They are half-citizens. Their rights exist in print but not in fact.

Illiterates cannot look up numbers in a telephone directory. Even if they can find the names of friends, few possess the sorting skills to make use of the yellow pages; categories are bewildering and trade names are beyond decoding capabilities for millions of nonreaders. Even the emergency numbers listed on the first page of the phone book—"Ambulance," "Police," and "Fire"—are too frequently beyond the recognition of nonreaders.

Many illiterates cannot read the admonition on a pack of cigarettes. Neither the Surgeon General's warning nor its reproduction on the package can alert them to the risks. Although most people learn by word of mouth that smoking is related to a number of grave physical disorders, they do not get the chance to read the detailed stories which can document this danger with the vividness that turns concern into determination to resist. They can see the handsome cowboy or the slim Virginia lady lighting up a filter cigarette; they cannot heed the words that tell them that this product is (not "may be") dangerous to their health. Sixty million men and women are condemned to be the unalerted, high-risk candidates for cancer.

Illiterates do not buy "no-name" products in the supermarkets. 20 They must depend on photographs or the familiar logos that are printed on the packages of brand-name groceries. The poorest people, therefore, are denied the benefits of the least costly products.

Illiterates depend almost entirely upon label recognition. Many labels, however, are not easy to distinguish. Dozens of different kinds of Campbell's soup appear identical to the nonreader. The purchaser who cannot read and does not dare to ask for help, out of the fear of being stigmatized (a fear which is unfortunately realistic), frequently comes home with something which she never wanted and her family never tasted.

Illiterates cannot read instructions on a pack of frozen food. Packages sometimes provide an illustration to explain the cooking preparations; but illustrations are of little help to someone who must "boil water, drop the food—*within* its plastic wrapper—in the boiling water, wait for it to simmer, instantly remove."

Even when labels are seemingly clear, they may be easily mistaken. A woman in Detroit brought home a gallon of Crisco for her children's dinner. She thought that she had bought the chicken that was pictured on the label. She had enough Crisco now to last a year—but no more money to go back and buy the food for dinner.

Recipes provided on the packages of certain staples sometimes tempt a semiliterate person to prepare a meal her children have not tasted. The longing to vary the uniform and often starchy content of low-budget meals provided to the family that relies on food stamps commonly leads to ruinous results. Scarce funds have been wasted and the food must be thrown out. The same applies to distribution of food-surplus produce in emergency conditions. Government inducements to poor people to "explore the ways" by which to make a tasty meal from tasteless noodles, surplus cheese, and powdered milk are useless to nonreaders. Intended as benevolent advice, such recommendations mock reality and foster deeper feelings of resentment and of inability to cope. (Those, on the other hand, who cautiously refrain from "innovative" recipes in preparation of their children's meals must suffer the opprobrium of "laziness," "lack of imagination . . .")

Illiterates cannot travel freely. When they attempt to do so, they 25 encounter risks that few of us can dream of. They cannot read traffic signs and, while they often learn to recognize and to decipher symbols, they cannot manage street names which they haven't seen before. The same is true for bus and subway stops. While ingenuity can sometimes help a man or woman to discern directions from familiar landmarks, buildings, cemeteries, churches, and the like, most illiterates are virtually immobilized. They seldom wander past the streets and neighborhoods they know. Geographical paralysis becomes a bitter metaphor for their entire existence. They are immobilized in almost every sense we can imagine. They can't move up. They can't move out. They cannot see beyond. Illiterates may take an oral test for drivers' permits in most sections of America. It is a questionable concession. Where will they go? How will they get there? How will they get home? Could it be that some of us might like it better if they stayed where they belong?

Travel is only one of many instances of circumscribed existence. Choice, in almost all its facets, is diminished in the life of an illiterate adult. Even the printed TV schedule, which provides most people with the luxury of preselection, does not belong within the arsenal of options in illiterate existence. One consequence is that the viewer watches only what appears at moments when he happens to have time to turn the switch. Another consequence, a lot more common, is that the TV set remains in operation night and day. Whatever the program offered at the hour when he walks into the room will be the nutriment that he accepts and swallows. Thus, to passivity, is added frequency—

indeed, almost uninterrupted continuity. Freedom to select is no more possible here than in the choice of home or surgery or food.

"You don't choose," said one illiterate woman. "You take your wishes from somebody else." Whether in perusal of a menu, selection of highways, purchase of groceries, or determination of affordable enjoyment, illiterate Americans must trust somebody else: a friend, a relative, a stranger on the street, a grocery clerk, a TV copywriter.

"All of our mail we get, it's hard for her to read. Settin' down and writing a letter, she can't do it. Like if we get a bill . . . we take it over to my sister-in-law . . . My sister-in-law reads it."

Billing agencies harass poor people for the payment of the bills for purchases that might have taken place six months before. Utility companies offer an agreement for a staggered payment schedule on a bill past due. "You have to trust them," one man said. Precisely for this reason, you end up by trusting no one and suspecting everyone of possible deceit. A submerged sense of distrust becomes the corollary to a constant need to trust. "They are cheating me . . . I have been tricked . . . I do not know . . ."

Not knowing: This is a familiar theme. Not knowing the right word 30 for the right thing at the right time is one form of subjugation. Not knowing the world that lies concealed behind those words is a more terrifying feeling. The longitude and latitude of one's existence are beyond all easy apprehension. Even the hard, cold stars within the firmament above one's head begin to mock the possibilities for self-location. Where am I? Where did I come from? Where will I go?

"I've lost a lot of jobs," one man explains. "Today, even if you're a janitor, there's still reading and writing . . . They leave a note saying, 'Go to room so-and-so . . .' You can't do it. You can't read it. You don't know."

"The hardest thing about it is that I've been places where I didn't know where I was. You don't know where you are . . . You're lost."

"Like I said: I have two kids. What do I do if one of my kids starts choking? I go running to the phone . . . I can't look up the hospital phone number. That's if we're at home. Out on the street, I can't read the sign. I get to a pay phone. 'Okay, tell us where you are. We'll send an ambulance.' I look at the street sign. Right there, I can't tell you what it says. I'd have to spell it out, letter for letter. By that time, one of my kids would be dead . . . These are the kinds of fears you go with, every single day . . ."

"Reading directions, I suffer with. I work with chemicals . . . That's scary to begin with . . ."

"You sit down. They throw the menu in front of you. Where do you go from there? Nine times out of ten you say, 'Go ahead. Pick out something for the both of us.' I've eaten some weird things, let me tell you!" 35

Menus. Chemicals. A child choking while his mother searches for a word she does not know to find assistance that will come too late. Another mother speaks about the inability to help her kids to read: "I can't read to them. Of course that's leaving them out of something they should have. Oh, it matters. You *believe* it matters! I ordered all these books. The kids belong to a book club. Donny wanted me to read a book to him. I told Donny: 'I can't read.' He said: 'Mommy, you sit down. I'll read it to you.' I tried it one day, reading from the pictures. Donny looked at me. He said, 'Mommy, that's not right.' He's only five. He knew I couldn't read . . ."

A landlord tells a woman that her lease allows him to evict her if her baby cries and causes inconvenience to her neighbors. The consequence of challenging his words conveys a danger which appears, unlikely as it seems, even more alarming than the danger of eviction. Once she admits that she can't read, in the desire to maneuver for the time in which to call a friend, she will have defined herself in terms of an explicit impotence that she cannot endure. Capitulation in this case is preferable to self-humiliation. Resisting the definition of oneself in terms of what one cannot do, what others take for granted, represents a need so great that other imperatives (even one so urgent as the need to keep one's home in winter's cold) evaporate and fall away in face of fear. Even the loss of home and shelter, in this case, is not so terrifying as the loss of self.

"I come out of school. I was sixteen. They had their meetings. The directors meet. They said that I was wasting their school paper. I was wasting pencils . . ."

Another illiterate, looking back, believes she was not worthy of her teacher's time. She believes that it was wrong of her to take up space within her school. She believes that it was right to leave in order that somebody more deserving could receive her place.

Children choke. Their mother chokes another way: on more than   40
chicken bones.

People eat what others order, know what others tell them, struggle not to see themselves as they believe the world perceives them. A man in California speaks about his own loss of identity, of self-location, definition:

"I stood at the bottom of the ramp. My car had broke down on the freeway. There was a phone. I asked for the police. They was nice. They said to tell them where I was. I looked up at the signs. There was one that I had seen before. I read it to them: ONE WAY STREET. They thought it was a joke. I told them I couldn't read. There was other signs above the ramp. They told me to try. I looked around for somebody to help. All the cars was going by real fast. I couldn't make them understand that I was lost. The cop was nice. He told me: 'Try once more.' I did my best. I couldn't read. I only knew the sign above my head. The cop was trying to be nice. He knew that I was trapped. 'I can't send out a car to you if you can't tell me where you are.' I felt afraid. I nearly cried. I'm forty-eight years old. I only said: 'I'm on a one-way street . . .' "

The legal problems and the courtroom complications that confront illiterate adults have been discussed above. The anguish that may underlie such matters was brought home to me this year while I was working on this book. I have spoken, in the introduction, of a sudden phone call from one of my former students, now in prison for a criminal offense. Stephen is not a boy today. He is twenty-eight years old. He called to ask me to assist him in his trial, which comes up next fall. He will be on trial for murder. He has just knifed and killed a man who first enticed him to his home, then cheated him, and then insulted him—as "an illiterate subhuman."

Stephen now faces twenty years to life. Stephen's mother was illiterate. His grandparents were illiterate as well. What parental curse did not destroy was killed off finally by the schools. Silent violence is repaid with interest. It will cost us $25,000 yearly to maintain this broken soul in prison. But what is the price that has been paid by Stephen's victim? What is the price that will be paid by Stephen?

Perhaps we might slow down a moment here and look at the realities 45 described above. This is the nation that we live in. This is a society that most of us did not create but which our president and other leaders have been willing to sustain by virtue of malign neglect. Do we possess the character and courage to address a problem which so many nations, poorer than our own, have found it natural to correct?

The answers to these questions represent a reasonable test of our belief in the democracy to which we have been asked in public school to swear allegiance.

STUDY QUESTIONS

1. Name one of the results of illiteracy that Kozol mentions. What effects does it have on an illiterate person's life? Cite a specific example Kozol gives of these effects in one person's life.

2. Why do you think Kozol includes so many examples in his essay? How would his essay have been different without them? Do you find them effective? Why or why not?

3. What is Kozol's THESIS? What is he trying to convince his readers to believe and/or do?

4. *For Writing.* Near the end of this chapter, Kozol asks, "Do we possess the character and courage to address a problem which so many nations, poorer than our own, have found it natural to correct?" In the decades since this piece was published in 1986, how successfully has America addressed the problem of illiteracy? Conduct RESEARCH and write an essay about American efforts to combat illiteracy. Include EVIDENCE to support your claim, and remember to document your sources.

ROBIN LAKOFF { *You Are What You Say*

ROBIN LAKOFF (b. 1942) earned her PhD in linguistics from Harvard University in 1967 and is presently a professor of sociolinguistics at the University of California, Berkeley. She is best known for her research into women's language; her groundbreaking work *Language and Woman's Place* (1975) identified many hallmarks of women's speech, including hedging phrases (*kind of, sort of*), apologies, and tag questions (*isn't it? aren't we?*). Among her other professional interests, Lakoff studies the interaction between politics and language, analyzing, for example, the speaking styles of Sarah Palin, John McCain, and Barack Obama during the 2008 presidential election, and publishing *The Language War* (2000), which explores the ways language is involved in power struggles.

Lakoff's 1974 essay "You Are What You Say," an early example of her writing on women's language, offers a capsule view of her theories. Comparing and contrasting the language used by and about men and women, Lakoff finds that women's speech patterns tend to make them seem tentative and submissive while words like "lady" and "girl" imply frivolousness and irresponsibility. As you read, notice the many examples Lakoff uses to support and illustrate her argument. Do you think the power dynamics between men and women changed since Lakoff penned this article in the early days of the feminist movement?

<hr>

"WOMEN'S LANGUAGE" IS THAT PLEASANT (dainty?), euphemistic, never-aggressive way of talking we learned as little girls. Cultural bias was built into the language we were allowed to speak, the subjects we were allowed to speak about, and the ways we were spoken of. Having learned our linguistic lesson well, we go out in the world, only to discover that we are communicative cripples—damned if we do, and damned if we don't.

If we refuse to talk "like a lady," we are ridiculed and criticized for being unfeminine. ("She thinks like a man" is, at best, a left-handed compliment.) If we do learn all the fuzzy-headed, unassertive language of our sex, we are ridiculed for being unable to think clearly, unable to take part in a serious discussion, and therefore unfit to hold a position of power.

It doesn't take much of this for a woman to begin feeling she deserves such treatment because of inadequacies in her own intelligence and education.

"Women's language" shows up in all levels of English. For example, women are encouraged and allowed to make far more precise discriminations in naming colors than men do. Words like *mauve, beige, ecru, aquamarine, lavender,* and so on, are unremarkable in a woman's active vocabulary, but largely absent from that of most men. I know of no evidence suggesting that women actually *see* a wider range of colors than men do. It is simply that fine discriminations of this sort are relevant to women's vocabularies, but not to men's; to men, who control most of the interesting affairs of the world, such distinctions are trivial—irrelevant.

In the area of syntax, we find similar gender-related peculiarities of speech. There is one construction, in particular, that women use conversationally far more than men: the tag-question. A tag is midway between an outright statement and a yes-no question; it is less assertive than the former, but more confident than the latter.

A *flat statement* indicates confidence in the speaker's knowledge and is fairly certain to be believed; a *question* indicates a lack of knowledge on some point and implies that the gap in the speaker's knowledge can and will be remedied by an answer. For example, if, at a Little League game, I have had my glasses off, I can legitimately ask someone else: "Was the player out at third?" A *tag question,* being intermediate between statement and question, is used when the speaker is stating a claim, but lacks full confidence in the truth of that claim. So if I say, "Is

Joan here?" I will probably not be surprised if my respondent answers "no"; but if I say, "Joan is here, isn't she?" instead, chances are I am already biased in favor of a positive answer, wanting only confirmation. I still want a response, but I have enough knowledge (or think I have) to predict that response. A tag question, then, might be thought of as a statement that doesn't demand to be believed by anyone but the speaker, a way of giving leeway, of not forcing the addressee to go along with the views of the speaker.

Another common use of the tag-question is in small talk when the speaker is trying to elicit conversation: "Sure is hot here, isn't it?"

But in discussing personal feelings or opinions, only the speaker normally has any way of knowing the correct answer. Sentences such as "I have a headache, don't I?" are clearly ridiculous. But there are other examples where it is the speaker's opinions, rather than perceptions, for which corroboration is sought, as in "The situation in Southeast Asia is terrible, isn't it?"

While there are, of course, other possible interpretations of a sentence like this, one possibility is that the speaker has a particular answer in mind—"yes" or "no"—but is reluctant to state it baldly. This sort of tag question is much more apt to be used by women than by men in conversation. Why is this the case?

The tag question allows a speaker to avoid commitment, and 10 thereby avoid conflict with the addressee. The problem is that, by so doing, speakers may also give the impression of not really being sure of themselves, or looking to the addressee for confirmation of their views. This uncertainty is reinforced in more subliminal ways, too. There is a peculiar sentence intonation-pattern, used almost exclusively by women, as far as I know, which changes a declarative answer into a question. The effect of using the rising inflection typical of a yes-no question is to imply that the speaker is seeking confirmation, even though the speaker is clearly the only one who has the requisite information, which is why the question was put to her in the first place:

(Q)   When will dinner be ready?

(A)   Oh . . . around six o'clock . . . ?

It is as though the second speaker were saying, "Six o'clock—if that's okay with you, if you agree." The person being addressed is put in the position of having to provide confirmation. One likely consequence of this sort of speech-pattern in a woman is that, often unbeknownst to herself, the speaker builds a reputation of tentativeness, and others will refrain from taking her seriously or trusting her with any real responsibilities, since she "can't make up her mind," and "isn't sure of herself."

Such idiosyncrasies may explain why women's language sounds much more "polite" than men's. It is polite to leave a decision open, not impose your mind, or views, or claims, on anyone else. So a tag-question is a kind of polite statement, in that it does not force agreement or belief on the addressee. In the same way a request is a polite command, in that it does not force obedience on the addressee, but rather suggests something be done as a favor to the speaker. A clearly stated order implies a threat of certain consequences if it is not followed, and—even more impolite—implies that the speaker is in a superior position and able to enforce the order. By couching wishes in the form of a request, on the other hand, a speaker implies that if the request is not carried out, only the speaker will suffer; noncompliance cannot harm the addressee. So the decision is really left up to addressee. The distinction becomes clear in these examples:

Close the door.

Please close the door.

Will you close the door?

Will you please close the door?

Won't you close the door?

In the same ways as words and speech patterns used *by* women undermine her image, those used *to describe* women make matters even worse. Often a word may be used of both men and women (and perhaps of things as well); but when it is applied to women, it assumes a special meaning that, by implication rather than outright assertion, is derogatory to women as a group.

The use of euphemisms has this effect. A euphemism is a substitute for a word that has acquired a bad connotation by association with something unpleasant or embarrassing. But almost as soon as the new word comes into common usage, it takes on the same old bad connotations, since feelings about the things or people referred to are not altered by a change of name; thus new euphemisms must be constantly found.

There is one euphemism for *woman* still very much alive. The word, of course, is *lady*. *Lady* has a masculine counterpart, namely *gentleman,* occasionally shortened to *gent.* But for some reason *lady* is very much commoner than *gentleman).*

The decision to use *lady* rather than *woman,* or vice versa, may considerably alter the sense of a sentence, as the following examples show: 15

(a)   A woman (lady) I know is a dean at Berkeley.

(b)   A woman (lady) I know makes amazing things out of shoe-
laces and old boxes.

The use of *lady* in (a) imparts a frivolous, or nonserious, tone to the sentence: the matter under discussion is not one of great moment. Similarly, in (b), using *lady* here would suggest that the speaker considered the "amazing things" not to be serious art, but merely a hobby or an aberration. If *woman* is used, she might be a serious sculptor. To say *lady doctor* is very condescending, since no one ever says *gentleman doctor* or even *man doctor.* For example, mention in the *San Francisco Chronicle* of January 31, 1972, of Madalyn Murray O'Hair as the *lady atheist* reduces her position to that of scatterbrained eccentric. Even *woman atheist* is scarcely defensible: sex is irrelevant to her philosophical position.

Many women argue that, on the other hand, *lady* carries with it overtones recalling the age of chivalry: conferring exalted stature on the person so referred to. This makes the term seem polite at first, but we must also remember that these implications are perilous: they suggest that a "lady" is helpless, and cannot do things by herself.

Lady can also be used to infer frivolousness, as in titles of organizations. Those that have a serious purpose (not merely that of enabling "the ladies" to spend time with one another) cannot use the word *lady* in their titles, but less serious ones may. Compare the *Ladies' Auxiliary* of a men's group, or the *Thursday Evening Ladies' Browning and Garden Society* with *Ladies' Liberation* or *Ladies' Strike for Peace.*

What is curious about this split is that *lady* is in origin a euphemism—a substitute that puts a better face on something people find uncomfortable—for *woman*. What kind of euphemism is it that subtly denigrates the people to whom it refers? Perhaps *lady* functions as a euphemism for *woman* because it does not contain the sexual implications present in *woman*: it is not "embarrassing" in that way. If this is so, we may expect that, in the future, *lady* will replace woman as the primary word for the human female, since *woman* will have become too blatantly sexual. That this distinction is already made in some contexts at least is shown in the following examples, where you can try replacing *woman* with *lady*:

(a)   She's only twelve, but she's already a woman.

(b)   After ten years in jail, Harry wanted to find a woman.

(c)   She's my woman, see, so don't mess around with her.

Another common substitute for *woman* is *girl*. One seldom hears a   20
man past the age of adolescence referred to as a boy, save in expressions like "going out with the boys," which are meant to suggest an air of adolescent frivolity and irresponsibility. But women of all ages are "girls": one can have a man—not a boy—Friday, but only a girl—never a woman or even a lady—Friday; women have girlfriends, but men do not—in a nonsexual sense—have boyfriends. It may be that this use of *girl* is euphemistic in the same way the use of *lady* is: in stressing the idea of immaturity, it removes the sexual connotations lurking in *woman*. *Girl* brings to mind irresponsibility: you don't send a girl to do a woman's errand (or even, for that matter, a boy's errand). She is a person who is both too immature and too far from real life to be entrusted with responsibilities or with decisions of any serious or important nature.

Now let's take a pair of words which, in terms of the possible relationships in an earlier society, were simple male-female equivalents, analogous to *bull : cow.* Suppose we find that, for independent reasons, society has changed in such a way that the original meanings now are irrelevant. Yet the words have not been discarded, but have acquired new meanings, metaphorically related to their original senses. But suppose these new metaphorical uses are no longer parallel to each other. By seeing where the parallelism breaks down, we discover something about the different roles played by men and women in this culture. One good example of such a divergence through time is found in the pair *master : mistress.* Once used with reference to one's power over servants, these words have become unusable today in their original master-servant sense as the relationship has become less prevalent in our society. But the words are still common.

Unless used with reference to animals, *master* now generally refers to a man who has acquired consummate ability in some field, normally nonsexual. But its feminine counterpart cannot be used this way. It is practically restricted to its sexual sense of "paramour." We start out with two terms, both roughly paraphrasable as "one who has power over another." But the masculine form, once one person is no longer able to have absolute power over another, becomes usable metaphorically in the sense of "having power over *something.*" *Master* requires as its object only the name of some activity, something inanimate and abstract. But *mistress* requires a masculine noun in the possessive to precede it. One cannot say: "Rhonda is a mistress." One must be *someone's* mistress. A man is defined by what he does, a woman by her sexuality, that is, in terms of one particular aspect of her relationship to men. It is one thing to be an *old master* like Hans Holbein, and another to be an *old mistress.*

The same is true of the words *spinster* and *bachelor*—gender words for "one who is not married." The resemblance ends with the definition. While *bachelor* is a neuter term, often used as a compliment, *spinster* normally is used pejoratively, with connotations of prissiness, fussiness, and so on. To be a bachelor implies that one has the choice of marrying or not, and this is what makes the idea of a bachelor existence attractive, in the popular literature. He has been pursued and has successfully eluded his pursuers. But a spinster is one who has not been pursued, or at least not seriously. She is old, unwanted goods. The metaphorical con-

LAKOFF / *You Are What You Say*

notations of *bachelor* generally suggest sexual freedom; of *spinster,* puritanism or celibacy.

These examples could be multiplied. It is generally considered a *faux pas,* in society, to congratulate a woman on her engagement, while it is correct to congratulate her fiancé. Why is this? The reason seems to be that it is impolite to remind people of things that may be uncomfortable to them. To congratulate a woman on her engagement is really to say, "Thank goodness! You had a close call!" For the man, on the other hand, there was no such danger. His choosing to marry is viewed as a good thing, but not something essential.

The linguistic double standard holds throughout the life of the relationship. After marriage, bachelor and spinster become man and wife, not man and woman. The woman whose husband dies remains "John's widow"; John, however, is never "Mary's widower." 25

Finally, why is it that salesclerks and others are so quick to call women customers "dear," "honey," and other terms of endearment they really have no business using? A male customer would never put up with it. But women, like children, are supposed to enjoy these endearments, rather than being offended by them.

In more ways than one, it's time to speak up.

STUDY QUESTIONS

1. How does Lakoff distinguish between the ways that women and men DESCRIBE colors or ask questions? How does she say men's and women's CONTRASTING styles of speaking are indicative of their relative power in society? How much of her ANALYSIS still seems relevant today? How much seems out of date?

2. In this essay, first published in 1974, Lakoff DEFINES some terms that are full of political innuendo: *lady, woman, girl, spinster, bachelor*. What STRATEGIES does she use to define them? What could you, more than thirty years later, add to these definitions?

3. *For Writing.* In the years since Lakoff wrote this essay, numerous other terms to describe women and men have entered the lexicon: *chick/dude* and *cougar/buck*, for instance. Choose one of these pairs (or suggest one yourself) and write an essay in which you define your terms and analyze their social implications. Do these contemporary slang terms convey the same underlying power dynamics that Lakoff describes in "You Are What You Say"?

WILLIAM LUTZ   { *The World of Doublespeak*

WILLIAM LUTZ (b. 1941) earned an MA from Marquette University, a PhD from the University of Nevada, Reno, and a JD from the Rutgers School of Law. He began teaching English at Rutgers in 1971 and is now an emeritus faculty member there. As a leader in the "plain language" movement, he has shared his expertise on radio and television programs, served as an expert legal witness on readability, and worked with private businesses and government agencies to make their information more accessible. Lutz has published more than two dozen articles in magazines and newspapers, including the *Los Angeles Times*, the *Atlanta Constitution*, the *Baltimore Sun*, *USA Today*, *Esquire*, and *The Times of London*. He has authored, co-authored, or edited several books, and he edited the *Quarterly Review of Doublespeak* for fourteen years. In 1996 the National Council of Teachers of English honored Lutz with the George Orwell Award for Distinguished Contribution to Honesty and Clarity in Public Language.

"The World of Doublespeak," the introductory chapter to Lutz's book *Doublespeak: From "Revenue Enhancement" to "Terminal Living"—How Government, Business, Advertisers, and Others Use Language to Deceive You* (1989), lays the foundation for much of Lutz's later work. In this excerpt from it, he defines "doublespeak" and identifies several of its major sources. While reading, think of examples of doublespeak you encounter today. What is the effect on the reader or listener of such language?

THERE ARE NO POTHOLES IN the streets of Tucson, Arizona, just "pavement deficiencies." The Reagan Administration didn't propose any new taxes, just "revenue enhancement" through new "user's fees."

Those aren't bums on the street, just "non-goal oriented members of society." There are no more poor people, just "fiscal underachievers." There was no robbery of an automatic teller machine, just an "unauthorized withdrawal." The patient didn't die because of medical malpractice, it was just a "diagnostic misadventure of a high magnitude." The U.S. Army doesn't kill the enemy anymore, it just "services the target." And the doublespeak goes on.

Doublespeak is language that pretends to communicate but really doesn't. It is language that makes the bad seem good, the negative appear positive, the unpleasant appear attractive or at least tolerable. Doublespeak is language that avoids or shifts responsibility, language that is at variance with its real or purported meaning. It is language that conceals or prevents thought; rather than extending thought, doublespeak limits it.

Doublespeak is not a matter of subjects and verbs agreeing; it is a matter of words and facts agreeing. Basic to doublespeak is incongruity, the incongruity between what is said or left unsaid, and what really is. It is the incongruity between the word and the referent, between seem and be, between the essential function of language—communication—and what doublespeak does—mislead, distort, deceive, inflate, circumvent, obfuscate.

HOW TO SPOT DOUBLESPEAK

How can you spot doublespeak? Most of the time you will recognize doublespeak when you see or hear it. But, if you have any doubts, you can identify doublespeak just by answering these questions: Who is saying what to whom, under what conditions and circumstances, with what intent, and with what results? Answering these questions will usually help you identify as doublespeak language that appears to be legitimate or that at first glance doesn't even appear to be doublespeak.

First Kind of Doublespeak

There are at least four kinds of doublespeak. The first is the euphemism, an inoffensive or positive word or phrase used to avoid a harsh, 5 unpleasant, or distasteful reality. But a euphemism can also be a tactful word or phrase which avoids directly mentioning a painful reality, or it can be an expression used out of concern for the feelings of someone else, or to avoid directly discussing a topic subject to a social or cultural taboo.

When you use a euphemism because of your sensitivity for someone's feelings or out of concern for a recognized social or cultural taboo, it is not doublespeak. For example, you express your condolences that someone has "passed away" because you do not want to say to a grieving person, "I'm sorry your father is dead." When you use the euphemism "passed away," no one is misled. Moreover, the euphemism functions here not just to protect the feelings of another person, but to communicate also your concern for that person's feelings during a period of mourning. When you excuse yourself to go to the "rest room," or you mention that someone is "sleeping with" or "involved with" someone else, you do not mislead anyone about your meaning, but you do respect the social taboos about discussing bodily functions and sex in direct terms. You also indicate your sensitivity to the feelings of your audience, which is usually considered a mark of courtesy and good manners.

However, when a euphemism is used to mislead or deceive, it becomes doublespeak. For example, in 1984 the U.S. State Department announced that it would no longer use the word "killing" in its annual report on the status of human rights in countries around the world. Instead, it would use the phrase "unlawful or arbitrary deprivation of life," which the department claimed was more accurate. Its real purpose for using this phrase was simply to avoid discussing the embarrassing situation of government-sanctioned killings in countries that are supported by the United States and have been certified by the United States as respecting the human rights of their citizens. This use of a euphemism constitutes doublespeak, since it is designed to mislead, to cover up the unpleasant. Its real intent is at variance with its apparent intent. It is language designed to alter our perception of reality.

The Pentagon, too, avoids discussing unpleasant realities when it refers to bombs and artillery shells that fall on civilian targets as "incontinent ordnance." And in 1977 the Pentagon tried to slip funding for the neutron bomb unnoticed into an appropriations bill by calling it a "radiation enhancement device."

Second Kind of Doublespeak

A second kind of doublespeak is jargon, the specialized language of a trade, profession, or similar group, such as that used by doctors, lawyers, engineers, educators, or car mechanics. Jargon can serve an important and useful function. Within a group, jargon functions as a kind of verbal shorthand that allows members of the group to communicate with each other clearly, efficiently, and quickly. Indeed, it is a mark of membership in the group to be able to use and understand the group's jargon.

But jargon, like the euphemism, can also be doublespeak. It can   10
be—and often is—pretentious, obscure, and esoteric terminology used to give an air of profundity, authority, and prestige to speakers and their subject matter. Jargon as doublespeak often makes the simple appear complex, the ordinary profound, the obvious insightful. In this sense it is used not to express but impress. With such doublespeak, the act of smelling something becomes "organoleptic analysis," glass becomes "fused silicate," a crack in a metal support beam becomes a "discontinuity," conservative economic policies become "distributionally conservative notions."

Lawyers, for example, speak of an "involuntary conversion" of property when discussing the loss or destruction of property through theft, accident, or condemnation. If your house burns down or if your car is stolen, you have suffered an involuntary conversion of your property. When used by lawyers in a legal situation, such jargon is a legitimate use of language, since lawyers can be expected to understand the term.

However, when a member of a specialized group uses its jargon to communicate with a person outside the group, and uses it knowing that the nonmember does not understand such language, then there is doublespeak. For example, on May 9, 1978, a National Airlines 727 airplane crashed while attempting to land at the Pensacola, Florida, airport. Three of the fifty-two passengers aboard the airplane were killed. As a result of the crash, National made an after-tax insurance benefit of $1.7 million, or an extra 18¢ a share dividend for its stockholders. Now National Airlines had two problems: It did not want to talk about one of its airplanes crashing, and it had to account for the $1.7 million when it issued its annual report to its stockholders. National solved the problem by inserting a footnote in its annual report which explained that the $1.7 million income was due to "the involuntary conversion of a 727." National thus acknowledged the crash of its airplane and the subsequent profit it made from the crash, without once mentioning the accident or the deaths. However, because airline officials knew that most stockholders in the company, and indeed most of the general public, were not familiar with legal jargon, the use of such jargon constituted doublespeak.

Third Kind of Doublespeak

A third kind of doublespeak is gobbledygook or bureaucratese. Basically, such doublespeak is simply a matter of piling on words, of overwhelming the audience with words, the bigger the words and the longer the sentences the better. Alan Greenspan, then chair of President Nixon's Council of Economic Advisors, was quoted in *The Philadelphia Inquirer* in 1974 as having testified before a Senate committee that "It is a tricky problem to find the particular calibration in timing that would be appropriate to stem the acceleration in risk premiums created by falling incomes without prematurely aborting the decline in the inflation-generated risk premiums."

Nor has Mr. Greenspan's language changed since then. Speaking to the meeting of the Economic Club of New York in 1988, Mr. Greenspan, now Federal Reserve chair, said, "I guess I should warn you, if I turn out to be particularly clear, you've probably misunderstood what I've said." Mr. Greenspan's doublespeak doesn't seem to have held back his career.

Sometimes gobbledygook may sound impressive, but when the 15 quote is later examined in print it doesn't even make sense. During the 1988 presidential campaign, vice-presidential candidate Senator Dan

Quayle explained the need for a strategic-defense initiative by saying, "Why wouldn't an enhanced deterrent, a more stable peace, a better prospect to denying the ones who enter conflict in the first place to have a reduction of offensive systems and an introduction to defensive capability? I believe this is the route the country will eventually go."

The investigation into the *Challenger* disaster in 1986[1] revealed the doublespeak of gobbledygook and bureaucratese used by too many involved in the shuttle program. When Jesse Moore, NASA's associate administrator, was asked if the performance of the shuttle program had improved with each launch or if it had remained the same, he answered, "I think our performance in terms of the liftoff performance and in terms of the orbital performance, we knew more about the envelope we were operating under, and we have been pretty accurately staying in that. And so I would say the performance has not by design drastically improved. I think we have been able to characterize the performance more as a function of our launch experience as opposed to it improving as a function of time." While this language may appear to be jargon, a close look will reveal that it is really just gobbledygook laced with jargon. But you really have to wonder if Mr. Moore had any idea what he was saying.

Fourth Kind of Doublespeak

The fourth kind of doublespeak is inflated language that is designed to make the ordinary seem extraordinary; to make everyday things seem impressive; to give an air of importance to people, situations, or things that would not normally be considered important; to make the simple seem complex. Often this kind of doublespeak isn't hard to spot, and it is usually pretty funny. While car mechanics may be called "automotive internists," elevator operators members of the "vertical transportation corps," used cars "pre-owned" or "experienced cars," and black-and-white television sets described as having "non-multicolor capability," you really aren't misled all that much by such language.

[1]The NASA space shuttle *Challenger* broke apart just after liftoff, killing all seven astronauts, including Christa McAuliffe, the first member of the Teacher in Space Project.

However, you may have trouble figuring out that, when Chrysler "initiates a career alternative enhancement program," it is really laying off five thousand workers; or that "negative patient care outcome" means the patient died; or that "rapid oxidation" means a fire in a nuclear power plant.

The doublespeak of inflated language can have serious consequences. In Pentagon doublespeak, "pre-emptive counterattack" means that American forces attacked first; "engaged the enemy on all sides" means American troops were ambushed; "backloading of augmentation personnel" means a retreat by American troops. In the doublespeak of the military, the 1983 invasion of Grenada was conducted not by the U.S. Army, Navy, Air Force, and Marines, but by the "Caribbean Peace Keeping Forces." But then, according to the Pentagon, it wasn't an invasion, it was a "predawn vertical insertion."

DOUBLESPEAK THROUGHOUT HISTORY

Doublespeak is not a new use of language peculiar to the politics or economics of the twentieth century. In the fifth century B.C., the Greek historian Thucydides wrote in *The Peloponnesian War* that 20

> revolution thus ran its course from city to city. . . . Words had to change their ordinary meanings and to take those which were now given them. Reckless audacity came to be considered the courage of a loyal ally; prudent hesitation, specious cowardice; moderation was held to be a cloak for unmanliness; ability to see all sides of a question, inaptness to act on any. Frantic violence became the attribute of manliness; cautious plotting, a justifiable means of self-defense. The advocate of extreme measures was always trustworthy; his opponent, a man to be suspected.

Julius Caesar, in his account of the Gallic Wars, described his brutal and bloody conquest and subjugation of Gaul as "pacifying" Gaul. "Where they make a desert, they call it peace," said an English nobleman quoted by the Roman historian Tacitus. When traitors were put to death in Rome, the announcement of their execution was made in

97

the form of saying "they have lived." "Taking notice of a man in the ancestral manner" meant capital punishment; "the prisoner was then led away" meant he was executed.

In his memoirs, *V-2*, Walter Dornberger, commanding officer of the Peenemünde Rocket Research Institute in Germany during World War II, describes how he and his staff used language to get what they needed from the Bureau of Budget for their rocket experiments. A pencil sharpener was an "Appliance for milling wooden dowels up to 10 millimeters in diameter," and a typewriter was an "Instrument for recording test data with rotating roller." But it was the Nazis who were the masters of doublespeak, and they used it not just to achieve and maintain power but to perpetrate some of the most heinous crimes in the history of the human race.

In the world of Nazi Germany, nonprofessional prostitutes were called "persons with varied sexual relationships"; "protective custody" was the very opposite of protective; "Winter Relief" was a compulsory tax presented as a voluntary charity; and a "straightening of the front" was a retreat, while serious difficulties became "bottlenecks." Minister of Information (the very title is doublespeak) Josef Goebbels spoke in all seriousness of "simple pomp" and "the liberalization of the freedom of the press."

Nazi doublespeak reached its peak when dealing with the "Final Solution,"[2] a phrase that is itself the ultimate in doublespeak. The notice, "The Jew X.Y. lived here," posted on a door, meant the occupant had been "deported," that is, killed. When mail was returned stamped "Addressee has moved away," it meant the person had been "deported." "Resettlement" also meant deportation, while "work camp" meant concentration camp or incinerator, "action" meant massacre, "Special Action Groups" were army units that conducted mass murder, "selection" meant gassing, and "shot while trying to escape" meant deliberately killed in a concentration camp.

---

[2] Adolf Hitler's plan to exterminate the Jewish population of Europe during World War II.

GEORGE ORWELL AND LANGUAGE

In his famous and now-classic essay, "Politics and the English 25
Language," which was published in 1946, George Orwell wrote that
the "great enemy of clear language is insincerity. When there is a gap
between one's real and one's declared aims, one turns as it were
instinctively to long words and exhausted idioms, like a cuttlefish
squirting out ink." For Orwell, language was an instrument for
"expressing and not for concealing or preventing thought." In his most
biting comment, he observed that, "in our time, political speech and
writing are largely the defense of the indefensible. . . . [P]olitical language has to consist largely of euphemism, question-begging, and
sheer cloudy vagueness. . . . Political language . . . is designed to make
lies sound truthful and murder respectable, and to give an appearance
of solidity to pure wind."

Orwell understood well the power of language as both a tool and a
weapon. In the nightmare world of his novel *1984,* Orwell depicted a
society where language was one of the most important tools of the
totalitarian state. Newspeak, the official state language in the world of
1984, was designed not to extend but to *diminish* the range of human
thought, to make only "correct" thought possible and all other modes
of thought impossible. It was, in short, a language designed to create a
reality that the state wanted.

Newspeak had another important function in Orwell's world of
1984. It provided the means of expression for doublethink, the mental
process that allows you to hold two opposing ideas in your mind at the
same time and believe in both of them. The classic example in Orwell's
novel is the slogan, "War Is Peace." Lest you think doublethink is confined only to Orwell's novel, you need only recall the words of
Secretary of State Alexander Haig when he testified before a congressional committee in 1982 that a continued weapons build-up by the
United States is "absolutely essential to our hopes for meaningful arms
reduction." Or remember what Senator Orrin Hatch said in 1988:
"Capital punishment is our society's recognition of the sanctity of
human life."

At its worst, doublespeak, like newspeak, is language designed to limit, if not eliminate, thought. Like doublethink, doublespeak enables speaker and listener, writer and reader, to hold two opposing ideas in their minds at the same time and believe in both of them. At its least offensive, doublespeak is inflated language that tries to give importance to the insignificant.[3]

*   *   *

DEADLY DOUBLESPEAK

There are instances, however, where doublespeak becomes more than amusing, more than a cause for a laugh. At St. Mary's Hospital in Minneapolis in 1982, an anesthetist turned the wrong knob during a Cesarean delivery, giving a fatal dose of nitrous oxide which killed the mother and unborn child. The hospital called it a "therapeutic misadventure." In its budget request to Congress in 1977, the Pentagon called the neutron bomb "an efficient nuclear weapon that eliminates an enemy with a minimum degree of damage to friendly territory." The Pentagon also calls the expected tens of millions of civilian dead in a nuclear war "collateral damage," a term the Pentagon also applies to the civilians killed in any war. And in 1977 people watching the Dick Cavett show on television learned from former Green Beret Captain Bob Marasco that during the Vietnam war the Central Intelligence Agency created the phrase "eliminate with extreme prejudice" to replace the more direct verb "kill."

President Reagan and the Doublespeak of Politics

Identifying doublespeak can at times be difficult. For example, on July   30
27, 1981, President Ronald Reagan said in a speech televised to the American public that "I will not stand by and see those of you who are

---

[3]To condense this selection the editors have omitted the next section of Lutz's chapter, titled "The Doublespeak All Around Us." In it, Lutz provides examples of doublespeak from three categories: the military, business, and education. Lutz concludes the section by remarking on the prevalance of doublespeak in education, citing this example from a 1966 research report from the U.S. Office of Education: "In other words feediness is the shared information between toputness, where toputness is at a time just prior to the inputness."

dependent on Social Security deprived of the benefits you've worked so hard to earn. You will continue to receive your checks in the full amount due you." This speech had been billed as President Reagan's position on Social Security, a subject of much debate at the time. After the speech, public opinion polls revealed that the great majority of the public believed that the president had affirmed his support for Social Security and that he would not support cuts in benefits. However, only days after the speech, on July 31, 1981, an article in the *Philadelphia Inquirer* quoted White House spokesperson David Gergen as saying that President Reagan's words had been "carefully chosen." What President Reagan had meant, according to Gergen, was that he was reserving the right to decide who was "dependent" on those benefits, who had "earned" them, and who, therefore, was "due" them.

The subsequent remarks of David Gergen reveal the real intent of President Reagan as opposed to his apparent intent. Thus, the criteria for analyzing language to determine whether it is doublespeak (who is saying what to whom, under what conditions and circumstances, with what intent, and with what results), when applied in light of David Gergen's remarks, reveal the doublespeak of President Reagan. Here, indeed, is the insincerity of which Orwell wrote. Here, too, is the gap between the speaker's real and declared aim.

Doublespeak and Political Advertisements

During the 1982 congressional election campaign, the Republican National Committee sponsored a television advertisement that pictured an elderly, folksy postman delivering Social Security checks "with the 7.4 percent cost-of-living raise that President Reagan promised." The postman then adds that "he promised that raise and he kept his promise, in spite of those sticks-in-the-mud who tried to keep him from doing what we elected him to do." The commercial was, in fact, deliberately misleading. The cost-of-living increases had been provided automatically by law since 1975, and President Reagan had tried three times to roll them back or delay them but was overruled by congressional opposition. When these discrepancies were pointed out to an official of the Republican National Committee, he called the com-

mercial "inoffensive" and added, "Since when is a commercial supposed to be accurate? Do women really smile when they clean their
ovens?"

Again, applying the criteria for identifying doublespeak to this
advertisement reveals the doublespeak in it, once you know the facts
of past actions by President Reagan. Moreover, the official for the
Republican National Committee assumes that all advertisements,
whether for political candidates or commercial products, do not tell
the truth; in his doublespeak, they do not have to be "accurate." Thus,
the real intent of the advertisement was to mislead, while the apparent
purpose of the commercial was to inform the public of President
Reagan's position on possible cuts in Social Security benefits. Again
there is insincerity, and again there is a gap between the speaker's real
and declared aims.

Alexander Haig and Doublespeak

One of the most chilling and terrifying uses of doublespeak in recent
memory occurred in 1981 when then Secretary of State Alexander
Haig was testifying before congressional committees about the murder
of three American nuns and a Catholic lay worker in El Salvador. The
four women had been raped and then shot at close range, and there
was clear evidence that the crime had been committed by soldiers
of the Salvadoran government. Before the House Foreign Affairs
Committee, Secretary Haig said:

> I'd like to suggest to you that some of the investigations would lead one
> to believe that perhaps the vehicle the nuns were riding in may have tried
> to run a roadblock, or may accidentally have been perceived to have
> been doing so, and there'd been an exchange of fire and then perhaps
> those who inflicted the casualties sought to cover it up. And this could
> have been at a very low level of both competence and motivation in the
> context of the issue itself. But the facts on this are not clear enough for
> anyone to draw a definitive conclusion.

The next day, before the Senate Foreign Relations Committee, 35
Secretary Haig claimed that press reports on his previous testimony

were "inaccurate." When Senator Claiborne Pell asked whether the secretary was suggesting the possibility that "the nuns may have run through a roadblock," he replied, "You mean that they tried to violate . . . ? Not at all, no, not at all. My heavens! The dear nuns who raised me in my parochial schooling would forever isolate me from their affections and respect." Then Senator Pell asked Secretary Haig, "Did you mean that the nuns were firing at the people, or what did 'an exchange of fire' mean?" The secretary replied, "I haven't met any pistol-packing nuns in my day, Senator. What I meant was that if one fellow starts shooting, then the next thing you know they all panic." Thus did the secretary of state of the United States explain official government policy on the murder of four American citizens in a foreign land.

Secretary Haig's testimony implies that the women were in some way responsible for their own fate. By using such vague wording as "would lead one to believe" and "may accidentally have been perceived to have been doing so," he avoids any direct assertion. The use of the phrase "inflicted the casualties" not only avoids using the word "kill" but also implies that at the worst the killings were accidental or justifiable. The result of this testimony is that the secretary of state has become an apologist for rape and murder. This is indeed language in defense of the indefensible; language designed to make lies sound truthful and murder respectable; language designed to give an appearance of solidity to pure wind.

THE DANGERS OF DOUBLESPEAK

These previous three examples of doublespeak should make it clear that doublespeak is not the product of carelessness or sloppy thinking. Indeed, most doublespeak is the product of clear thinking and is carefully designed and constructed to appear to communicate when in fact it doesn't. It is language designed not to lead but mislead. It is language designed to distort reality and corrupt thought. In the world created by doublespeak, if it's not a tax increase, but rather "revenue enhancement" or "tax base broadening," how can you complain about higher taxes? If it's not acid rain, but rather "poorly buffered precipitation," how can you worry about all those dead trees? If that isn't the Mafia in Atlantic City, but just "members of a career-offender cartel," why worry about the influence of organized crime in the city? If Supreme Court Justice William Rehnquist wasn't addicted to the pain-killing drug his doctor prescribed, but instead it was just that the drug had "established an interrelationship with the body, such that if the drug is removed precipitously, there is a reaction," you needn't question that his decisions might have been influenced by his drug addiction. If it's not a Titan II nuclear-armed intercontinental ballistic missile with a warhead 630 times more powerful than the atomic bomb dropped on Hiroshima, but instead, according to Air Force Colonel Frank Horton, it's just a "very large, potentially disruptive reentry system," why be concerned about the threat of nuclear destruction? Why worry about the neutron bomb escalating the arms race if it's just a "radiation enhancement weapon"? If it's not an invasion, but a "rescue mission" or a "predawn vertical insertion," you won't need to think about any violations of U.S. or international law.

Doublespeak has become so common in everyday living that many people fail to notice it. Even worse, when they do notice doublespeak being used on them, they don't react, they don't protest. Do you protest when you are asked to check your packages at the desk "for your convenience," when it's not for your convenience at all but for someone else's? You see advertisements for "genuine imitation leather," "virgin vinyl," or "real counterfeit diamonds," but do you question the language or the supposed quality of the product? Do you question politicians who don't speak of slums or ghettos but of the "inner city" or "substandard housing" where the "disadvantaged" live and thus avoid talking about the poor who have to live in filthy, poorly heated, ramshackle apartments or houses? Aren't you amazed that patients don't die in the hospital anymore, it's just "negative patient-care outcome"?

Doublespeak such as that noted earlier that defines cab drivers as "urban transportation specialists," elevator operators as members of the "vertical transportation corps," and automobile mechanics as "automotive internists" can be considered humorous and relatively harmless. However, when a fire in a nuclear reactor building is called "rapid oxidation," an explosion in a nuclear power plant is called an "energetic disassembly," the illegal overthrow of a legitimate government is termed "destabilizing a government," and lies are seen as "inoperative statements," we are hearing doublespeak that attempts to avoid responsibility and make the bad seem good, the negative appear positive, something unpleasant appear attractive; and which seems to communicate but doesn't. It is language designed to alter our perception of reality and corrupt our thinking. Such language does not provide us with the tools we need to develop, advance, and preserve our culture and our civilization. Such language breeds suspicion, cynicism, distrust, and, ultimately, hostility.

Doublespeak is insidious because it can infect and eventually 40 destroy the function of language, which is communication between people and social groups. This corruption of the function of language can have serious and far-reaching consequences. We live in a country that depends upon an informed electorate to make decisions in selecting candidates for office and deciding issues of public policy. The use of doublespeak can become so pervasive that it becomes the coin of the political realm, with speakers and listeners convinced that they really understand such language. After a while we may really believe that politicians don't lie but only "misspeak," that illegal acts are merely "inappropriate actions," that fraud and criminal conspiracy are just "miscertification." President Jimmy Carter in April of 1980 could call the aborted raid to free the American hostages in Teheran an "incomplete success" and really believe that he had made a statement that clearly communicated with the American public. So, too, could President Ronald Reagan say in 1985 that "ultimately our security and our hopes for success at the arms reduction talks hinge on the determination that we show here to continue our program to rebuild and refortify our defenses" and really believe that greatly increasing the amount of money spent building new weapons would lead to a reduction in the number of weapons in the world. If we really believe that we understand such language and that such language communicates and promotes clear thought, then the world of *1984,* with its control of reality through language, is upon us.

STUDY QUESTIONS

1. What exactly is "doublespeak"? Sum up Lutz's DEFINITION of this term in a single sentence.

2. Within this definition essay, Lutz makes the ARGUMENT that doublespeak can be dangerous and damaging. What EVIDENCE does he offer for this CLAIM? How effective do you find it? How does his extended definition of doublespeak support this idea?

3. Lutz wrote this essay as the first chapter to his book *Doublespeak* (1989). How might it have been different if he'd written it as a speech? As an op-ed piece? As a BLOG entry? What if he were writing today?

4. *For Writing.* Using Lutz's definition of doublespeak, find an example of doublespeak spoken or written in the last twelve months. In an essay, present your example, ANALYZE what makes it doublespeak, and consider what the intent might have been as well as the actual result.

MOTOKO RICH $\left\{\begin{array}{l} \textit{Literacy Debate: Online,} \\ \\ \textit{R U Really Reading?} \end{array}\right.$

MOTOKO RICH (b. 1970) was born in Los Angeles, California, but grew up primarily in Petaluma. She graduated from Yale University in 1991 and received an MA in English from Cambridge University. Rich was a reporter at the *Wall Street Journal* for six years before moving in 2003 to the *New York Times,* where she reviews books and writes about culture and the arts.

In "Literacy Debate: Online, R U Really Reading?" Rich presents proponents' and opponents' views about children and teenagers reading online. Education scholars and researchers correlate falling standardized test scores among children and teens and a drop in the percentage of teens who say they read for fun with the amount of time children and teens spend on computers. On the other hand, Web enthusiasts argue that the reading strategies gained through online reading prepare students for work in today's digital society, and that Internet proficiency should be tested in the same way students are tested in print material for reading comprehension. As you read, determine whether Rich draws any conclusions.

BOOKS ARE NOT NADIA KONYK'S thing. Her mother, hoping to entice her, brings them home from the library, but Nadia rarely shows an interest.

Instead, like so many other teenagers, Nadia, 15, is addicted to the Internet. She regularly spends at least six hours a day in front of the computer here in this suburb southwest of Cleveland.

A slender, chatty blonde who wears black-framed plastic glasses, Nadia checks her e-mail and peruses myyearbook.com, a social networking site, reading messages or posting updates on her mood. She searches for music videos on YouTube and logs onto Gaia Online, a role-playing site where members fashion alternate identities as cutesy cartoon characters. But she spends most of her time on quizilla.com or fanfiction.net, reading and commenting on stories written by other users and based on books, television shows or movies.

Her mother, Deborah Konyk, would prefer that Nadia, who gets A's and B's at school, read books for a change. But at this point, Ms. Konyk said, "I'm just pleased that she reads something anymore."

Children like Nadia lie at the heart of a passionate debate about just 5 what it means to read in the digital age. The discussion is playing out among educational policy makers and reading experts around the world, and within groups like the National Council of Teachers of English and the International Reading Association.

As teenagers' scores on standardized reading tests have declined or stagnated, some argue that the hours spent prowling the Internet are the enemy of reading—diminishing literacy, wrecking attention spans and destroying a precious common culture that exists only through the reading of books.

But others say the Internet has created a new kind of reading, one that schools and society should not discount. The Web inspires a teenager like Nadia, who might otherwise spend most of her leisure time watching television, to read and write.

Even accomplished book readers like Zachary Sims, 18, of Old Greenwich, Connecticut, crave the ability to quickly find different points of view on a subject and converse with others online. Some children with dyslexia or other learning difficulties, like Hunter Gaudet, 16, of Somers, Connecticut, have found it far more comfortable to search and read online.

At least since the invention of television, critics have warned that electronic media would destroy reading. What is different now, some literacy experts say, is that spending time on the Web, whether it is looking up something on Google or even britneyspears.org, entails some engagement with text.

SETTING EXPECTATIONS

Few who believe in the potential of the Web deny the value of books.   10
But they argue that it is unrealistic to expect all children to read *To Kill a Mockingbird* or *Pride and Prejudice* for fun. And those who prefer staring at a television or mashing buttons on a game console, they say, can still benefit from reading on the Internet. In fact, some literacy experts say that online reading skills will help children fare better when they begin looking for digital-age jobs.

Some Web evangelists say children should be evaluated for their proficiency on the Internet just as they are tested on their print reading comprehension. Starting next year, some countries will participate in new international assessments of digital literacy, but the United States, for now, will not.

Clearly, reading in print and on the Internet are different. On paper, text has a predetermined beginning, middle and end, where readers focus for a sustained period on one author's vision. On the Internet, readers skate through cyberspace at will and, in effect, compose their own beginnings, middles and ends.

Young people "aren't as troubled as some of us older folks are by reading that doesn't go in a line," said Rand J. Spiro, a professor of educational psychology at Michigan State University who is studying reading practices on the Internet. "That's a good thing because the world doesn't go in a line, and the world isn't organized into separate compartments or chapters."

Some traditionalists warn that digital reading is the intellectual equivalent of empty calories. Often, they argue, writers on the Internet employ a cryptic argot that vexes teachers and parents. Zigzagging through a cornucopia of words, pictures, video and sounds, they say, distracts more than strengthens readers. And many youths spend most of their time on the Internet playing games or sending instant messages, activities that involve minimal reading at best.

Last fall the National Endowment for the Arts issued a sobering report   15
linking flat or declining national reading test scores among teenagers with the slump in the proportion of adolescents who said they read for fun.

According to Department of Education data cited in the report, just over a fifth of 17-year-olds said they read almost every day for fun in 2004, down from nearly a third in 1984. Nineteen percent of 17-year-olds said they never or hardly ever read for fun in 2004, up from 9 percent in 1984. (It was unclear whether they thought of what they did on the Internet as "reading.")

"Whatever the benefits of newer electronic media," Dana Gioia, the chairman of the N.E.A., wrote in the report's introduction, "they provide no measurable substitute for the intellectual and personal development initiated and sustained by frequent reading."

Children are clearly spending more time on the Internet. In a study of 2,032 representative 8- to 18-year-olds, the Kaiser Family Foundation found that nearly half used the Internet on a typical day in 2004, up from just under a quarter in 1999. The average time these children spent online on a typical day rose to one hour and 41 minutes in 2004, from 46 minutes in 1999.

The question of how to value different kinds of reading is complicated because people read for many reasons. There is the level required of daily life—to follow the instructions in a manual or to analyze a mortgage contract. Then there is a more sophisticated level that opens the doors to elite education and professions. And, of course, people read for entertainment, as well as for intellectual or emotional rewards.

It is perhaps that final purpose that book champions emphasize 20 the most.

"Learning is not to be found on a printout," David McCullough, the Pulitzer Prize–winning biographer, said in a commencement address at Boston College in May. "It's not on call at the touch of the finger. Learning is acquired mainly from books, and most readily from great books."

WHAT'S BEST FOR NADIA?

Deborah Konyk always believed it was essential for Nadia and her 8-year-old sister, Yashca, to read books. She regularly read aloud to the girls and took them to library story hours.

"Reading opens up doors to places that you probably will never get to visit in your lifetime, to cultures, to worlds, to people," Ms. Konyk said.

Ms. Konyk, who took a part-time job at a dollar store chain a year and a half ago, said she did not have much time to read books herself. There are few books in the house. But after Yashca was born, Ms. Konyk spent the baby's nap time reading the Harry Potter novels to Nadia, and she regularly brought home new titles from the library.

Despite these efforts, Nadia never became a big reader. Instead, she became obsessed with Japanese anime cartoons on television and comics like "Sailor Moon." Then, when she was in the sixth grade, the family bought its first computer. When a friend introduced Nadia to fanfiction.net, she turned off the television and started reading online. 25

Now she regularly reads stories that run as long as 45 Web pages. Many of them have elliptical plots and are sprinkled with spelling and grammatical errors. One of her recent favorites was "My absolutely, perfect normal life . . . ARE YOU CRAZY? NOT!," a story based on the anime series "Beyblade."

In one scene the narrator, Aries, hitches a ride with some masked men and one of them pulls a knife on her. "Just then I notice (Like finally) something sharp right in front of me," Aries writes. "I gladly took it just like that until something terrible happen. . . ."

Nadia said she preferred reading stories online because "you could add your own character and twist it the way you want it to be."

"So like in the book somebody could die," she continued, "but you could make it so that person doesn't die or make it so like somebody else dies who you don't like."

Nadia also writes her own stories. She posted "Dieing Isn't Always 30 Bad," about a girl who comes back to life as half cat, half human, on both fanfiction.net and quizilla.com.

Nadia said she wanted to major in English at college and someday hopes to be published. She does not see a problem with reading few books. "No one's ever said you should read more books to get into college," she said.

The simplest argument for why children should read in their leisure time is that it makes them better readers. According to federal statistics, students who say they read for fun once a day score significantly higher on reading tests than those who say they never do.

Reading skills are also valued by employers. A 2006 survey by the Conference Board, which conducts research for business leaders, found that nearly 90 percent of employers rated "reading comprehension" as "very important" for workers with bachelor's degrees. Department of Education statistics also show that those who score higher on reading tests tend to earn higher incomes.

Critics of reading on the Internet say they see no evidence that increased Web activity improves reading achievement. "What we are losing in this country and presumably around the world is the sustained, focused, linear attention developed by reading," said Mr. Gioia of the N.E.A. "I would believe people who tell me that the Internet develops reading if I did not see such a universal decline in reading ability and reading comprehension on virtually all tests."

Nicholas Carr sounded a similar note in "Is Google Making Us 35 Stupid?" in the current issue of the *Atlantic* magazine. Warning that the Web was changing the way he—and others—think, he suggested that the effects of Internet reading extended beyond the falling test scores of adolescence. "What the Net seems to be doing is chipping away my capacity for concentration and contemplation," he wrote, confessing that he now found it difficult to read long books.

Literacy specialists are just beginning to investigate how reading on the Internet affects reading skills. A recent study of more than 700 low-income, mostly Hispanic and black sixth through 10th graders in Detroit found that those students read more on the Web than in any other medium, though they also read books. The only kind of reading that related to higher academic performance was frequent novel reading, which predicted better grades in English class and higher overall grade point averages.

Elizabeth Birr Moje, a professor at the University of Michigan who led the study, said novel reading was similar to what schools demand already. But on the Internet, she said, students are developing new reading skills that are neither taught nor evaluated in school.

One early study showed that giving home Internet access to low-income students appeared to improve standardized reading test scores and school grades. "These were kids who would typically not be reading in their free time," said Linda A. Jackson, a psychology professor at Michigan State who led the research. "Once they're on the Internet, they're reading."

Neurological studies show that learning to read changes the brain's circuitry. Scientists speculate that reading on the Internet may also affect the brain's hard wiring in a way that is different from book reading.

"The question is, does it change your brain in some beneficial way?" said Guinevere F. Eden, director of the Center for the Study of Learning at Georgetown University. "The brain is malleable and adapts to its environment. Whatever the pressures are on us to succeed, our brain will try and deal with it." 40

Some scientists worry that the fractured experience typical of the Internet could rob developing readers of crucial skills. "Reading a book, and taking the time to ruminate and make inferences and engage the imaginational processing, is more cognitively enriching, without doubt, than the short little bits that you might get if you're into the 30-second digital mode," said Ken Pugh, a cognitive neuroscientist at Yale who has studied brain scans of children reading.

BUT THIS IS READING TOO

Web proponents believe that strong readers on the Web may eventually surpass those who rely on books. Reading five Web sites, an op-ed article and a blog post or two, experts say, can be more enriching than reading one book.

"It takes a long time to read a 400-page book," said Mr. Spiro of Michigan State. "In a 10th of the time," he said, the Internet allows a reader to "cover a lot more of the topic from different points of view."

Zachary Sims, the Old Greenwich, Connecticut, teenager, often stays awake until 2 or 3 in the morning reading articles about technology or politics—his current passions—on up to 100 Web sites.

"On the Internet, you can hear from a bunch of people," said Zachary, who will attend Columbia University this fall. "They may not be pedigreed academics. They may be someone in their shed with a conspiracy theory. But you would weigh that." 45

Though he also likes to read books (earlier this year he finished, and loved, *The Fountainhead* by Ayn Rand), Zachary craves interaction with fellow readers on the Internet. "The Web is more about a conversation," he said. "Books are more one-way."

The kinds of skills Zachary has developed—locating information quickly and accurately, corroborating findings on multiple sites—may seem obvious to heavy Web users. But the skills can be cognitively demanding.

Web readers are persistently weak at judging whether information is trustworthy. In one study, Donald J. Leu, who researches literacy and technology at the University of Connecticut asked 48 students to look at a spoof Web site (http://zapatopi.net/treeoctopus/) about a mythical species known as the "Pacific Northwest tree octopus." Nearly 90 percent of them missed the joke and deemed the site a reliable source.

Some literacy experts say that reading itself should be redefined. Interpreting videos or pictures, they say, may be as important a skill as analyzing a novel or a poem.

"Kids are using sound and images so they have a world of ideas to put together that aren't necessarily language oriented," said Donna E. Alvermann, a professor of language and literacy education at the University of Georgia. "Books aren't out of the picture, but they're only one way of experiencing information in the world today." 50

A LIFELONG STRUGGLE

In the case of Hunter Gaudet, the Internet has helped him feel more comfortable with a new kind of reading. A varsity lacrosse player in Somers, Connecticut, Hunter has struggled most of his life to read. After learning he was dyslexic in the second grade, he was placed in special education classes and a tutor came to his home three hours a week. When he entered high school, he dropped the special education classes, but he still reads books only when forced, he said.

In a book, "they go through a lot of details that aren't really needed," Hunter said. "Online just gives you what you need, nothing more or less."

When researching the 19th-century Chief Justice Roger B. Taney for one class, he typed Taney's name into Google and scanned the Wikipedia entry and other biographical sites. Instead of reading an entire page, he would type in a search word like "college" to find Taney's alma mater, assembling his information nugget by nugget.

Experts on reading difficulties suggest that for struggling readers, the Web may be a better way to glean information. "When you read online there are always graphics," said Sally Shaywitz, the author of *Overcoming Dyslexia* and a Yale professor. "I think it's just more comfortable and—I hate to say easier—but it more meets the needs of somebody who might not be a fluent reader."

Karen Gaudet, Hunter's mother, a regional manager for a retail 55 chain who said she read two or three business books a week, hopes Hunter will eventually discover a love for books. But she is confident that he has the reading skills he needs to succeed.

"Based on where technology is going and the world is going," she said, "he's going to be able to leverage it."

When he was in seventh grade, Hunter was one of 89 students who participated in a study comparing performance on traditional state reading tests with a specially designed Internet reading test. Hunter, who scored in the lowest 10 percent on the traditional test, spent weeks learning how to use the Web for a science class before taking the Internet test. It was composed of three sets of directions asking the students to search for information online, determine which sites were reliable and explain their reasoning.

Hunter scored in the top quartile. In fact, about a third of the students in the study, led by Professor Leu, scored below average on traditional reading tests but did well on the Internet assessment.

THE TESTING DEBATE

To date, there have been few large-scale appraisals of Web skills. The Educational Testing Service, which administers the SAT, has developed a digital literacy test known as iSkills that requires students to solve informational problems by searching for answers on the Web. About 80 colleges and a handful of high schools have administered the test so far.

But according to Stephen Denis, product manager at ETS, of the   60
more than 20,000 students who have taken the iSkills test since 2006,
only 39 percent of four-year-college freshmen achieved a score that
represented "core functional levels" in Internet literacy.

Now some literacy experts want the federal tests known as the
nation's report card to include a digital reading component. So far,
the traditionalists have held sway: The next round, to be administered to fourth and eighth graders in 2009, will test only print reading
comprehension.

Mary Crovo of the National Assessment Governing Board, which
creates policies for the national tests, said several members of a committee that sets guidelines for the reading tests believed large numbers
of low-income and rural students might not have regular Internet access, rendering measurements of their online skills unfair.

Some simply argue that reading on the Internet is not something
that needs to be tested—or taught.

"Nobody has taught a single kid to text message," said Carol Jago of
the National Council of Teachers of English and a member of the testing guidelines committee. "Kids are smart. When they want to do
something, schools don't have to get involved."

Michael L. Kamil, a professor of education at Stanford who lobbied   65
for an Internet component as chairman of the reading test guidelines
committee, disagreed. Students "are going to grow up having to be
highly competent on the Internet," he said. "There's no reason to make
them discover how to be highly competent if we can teach them."

The United States is diverging from the policies of some other
countries. Next year, for the first time, the Organization for Economic
Cooperation and Development, which administers reading, math and
science tests to a sample of 15-year-old students in more than 50 countries, will add an electronic reading component. The United States,
among other countries, will not participate. A spokeswoman for the
Institute of Education Sciences, the research arm of the Department of
Education, said an additional test would overburden schools.

Even those who are most concerned about the preservation of
books acknowledge that children need a range of reading experiences.
"Some of it is the informal reading they get in e-mails or on Web sites,"

said Gay Ivey, a professor at James Madison University who focuses on adolescent literacy. "I think they need it all."

Web junkies can occasionally be swept up in a book. After Nadia read Elie Wiesel's Holocaust memoir *Night* in her freshman English class, Ms. Konyk brought home another Holocaust memoir, *I Have Lived a Thousand Years*, by Livia Bitton-Jackson.

Nadia was riveted by heartbreaking details of life in the concentration camps. "I was trying to imagine this and I was like, I can't do this," she said. "It was just so—wow."

Hoping to keep up the momentum, Ms. Konyk brought home an- 70 other book, *Silverboy*, a fantasy novel. Nadia made it through one chapter before she got engrossed in the Internet fan fiction again.

STUDY QUESTIONS

1. Rich begins and ends her article with PROFILES of particular teenagers; in between, she presents ARGUMENTS about the Internet's effect on reading. What is the relationship between the RESEARCH Rich cites and Nadia's and Zachary's reading experiences? How do the profiles of individuals contribute to the rest of the article?

2. What is the significance of the way the title is written? Does the title suggest the author's POSITION? Explain. Does the author provide a definitive answer to the question in the title? If so, what is it?

3. Rich sets up her essay as a Rogerian argument: one that presents multiple sides of an issue, from both proponents and opponents. Does she ever provide a CLAIM? Why or why not?

4. LIST the EVIDENCE that supports electronic media as a legitimate method of reading and the evidence that opposes it. Based on the evidence presented in the article, which side do you agree with—or do you find a middle ground? Write your own claim and be prepared to defend it in class.

5. *For Writing.* Write a LITERACY NARRATIVE about one or more early experiences you had reading in print and online. Include your attitude toward reading, your favorite reading material, and when and where you read. REFLECT on your enjoyment of reading or lack thereof—if you enjoyed reading, what did you enjoy about it? If you didn't, why didn't you?

DAVID SHIPLEY

AND WILL SCHWALBE

{

How to Write

(the Perfect) Email

DAVID SHIPLEY (b. 1963) is the Op-Ed editor of the *New York Times*.
From 1995 to 1997 he served the Clinton administration as a special assistant to the president and speechwriter. Prior to his White House experience,
he was the executive editor of the *New Republic*.

WILL SCHWALBE (b. 1962) works in the field of new media and served as
senior vice president and editor-in-chief of both Hyperion Books and
William Morrow. He is on the board of governors of Yale University Press.
Schwalbe has a background in journalism and has written for such pub-
lications as the *New York Times, Ms.* magazine, and the *South China
Morning Post*.

Shipley and Schwalbe collaborated on *Send: Why People Email So
Badly and How to Do It Better* (2007). In the following selection from
that book, the authors instruct readers on how to write the "perfect"
e-mail, taking into account such elements as word choice, spelling, grammar,
and emoticons. The key, they say, is to consider carefully your relationship
to the person who will receive your message. As you read these instructions,
think about the kind of e-mails that you send and receive on a daily basis.
Do they follow Shipley and Schwalbe's guidelines? If not, why not?

THE FACT THAT EMAIL IS a searchable, storable medium means that
you have to compose your message with special care. And the fact that
you are writing—constructing sentences, choosing words, making
grammatical decisions, adding punctuation—with previously unimag-
inable swiftness makes the situation all the more vexed, as does the

delusion that email, because it's electronic, is somehow more ephemeral than, say, a letter.

Also, because it's *often* acceptable to be lax about the rules of grammar on email, there's the misconception that it's *always* acceptable to be lax about them. That's not the case. We aren't going to offer a guide to style and usage here—lots of books have done that already and done it well. What we are going to do, though, is outline the implications of taking risks with your English in emails and review the stylistic traps that are peculiar to the medium.

CHOOSING THE RIGHT WORDS

In Japanese, the status of the person you are addressing governs the words you use. A sentence directed toward a peer, for instance, requires different word forms from one directed to someone higher or lower than you on the social ladder. (You use one word form when speaking to your boss, another to a colleague, yet another to a child.) Learning Japanese, then, requires learning multiple ways of saying the same thing. The need to remember which kind of word form to use is one of the elements that makes it hard for native English speakers to master Japanese.

What many people don't consider, however, is that in this respect English is arguably more complicated than Japanese—precisely because English doesn't offer the convenience of different words to signal that you know the nature of your social relationship to the person with whom you are speaking. In lieu of specific words to show deference—or familiarity—English relies heavily on the delicate manipulation of tone.

More than anything else, vocabulary conveys tone and reveals you 5 as boss or subordinate, buyer or seller, seeker or sage. The words you choose can be formal, casual, or somewhere in between; they can be literal or figurative; they can be precise or vague; understated, correct, or exaggerated; simple or complex; common or rare; prosaic or poetic; contracted or not.

Certainly, some words are inherently safer than others, but if you never venture beyond them you become yet another unmemorable correspondent, ceding the chance to make an impression in your email. Think of your own inbox. When wading through an ocean of emails, don't you yearn for one to jump out? After a hundred people email you that they "look forward to meeting you" so that they can share their "qualifications" or "describe the benefits of their product" or present you with a "business opportunity," you crave something by someone who took the time to choose words with personality, rather than simply cribbing phrases from the modern business lexicon. The trick is to be vivid and specific—even, perhaps, revealing—without forgetting your original relationship with the person to whom you're writing.

On the most elemental level, the deal is this. Before you set finger to keyboard, ask yourself one question (and don't write until you get the answer): *What is my relationship to the person I'm writing?* Then, make sure your word choice is appropriate.

*   *   *

MISSPELLINGS

If careful word choice is the ultimate goal, then accidental word choice is the ultimate pitfall. There is a big difference between poor spelling that reads as sloppiness and poor spelling that results in an entirely different word appearing from the one intended. As people have increasingly come to rely on computer spell-check programs, they've also become increasingly susceptible to creating documents where an entirely wrong, albeit correctly spelled, word has found its way into the text. When the word is obviously wrong ("sned," not "send"), then the recipient will probably guess correctly that you simply failed to proof the document. But when a word is more subtly wrong, then at best she may think you didn't know the meaning of the word you used; at worst she will assume the wrong word was the chosen one, and judge you accordingly.

A computer won't flag "affect" when you meant "effect." If you want your battery changed because it can no longer safely hold a charge, the ramifications if you accidentally ask for it to be charged instead of changed could be disastrous. Will once received an unintentionally

121

humorous note about a film called *The Dangerous Lives of Alter Boys,* except that "Alter" was supposed to be "Altar." The sender intended the Subject line to refer to helpful Catholic children and not castrati.

A friend once received an email that said: 10

> am in Pqris trying to flog q book or 3—bugger French keyboqrds and forgive the ,istqkes: Will e,qil you over the weekend: Clips qrrived todqy qnd very many thqnks.

This is actually a charming example of what would otherwise be a disastrous piece of correspondence. It's saved because its meaning is still clear, it was among pals, and the misspellings are both ubiquitous and cheerfully acknowledged. The point is not that you should never misspell a word, but that you should be aware of how it will be received when you do.

GRAMMAR

Grammar is as important in determining tone as word choice is. The very same words, in different combinations, may or may not mean the same thing. But even if they mean the same thing, they may or may not convey the same tone. The examples used here aren't confined to email because good writing is good writing, no matter the medium.

Bad grammar isn't always wrong. "It ain't over till it's over" isn't right, but it's both memorable and effective. But even good grammar has its pitfalls. A simple sentence can be direct and unvarnished and perfectly appropriate. Or it can come across as childish or dictatorial. A complex sentence can sound conversational or elegant; it can also seem blathering or pompous.

Here's how simple grammar can be used to great effect.

On February 15, 1963, President John F. Kennedy wrote the following memo to Robert McNamara, his secretary of defense, after he had learned that the new military attaché to Laos, a former French colony, had only limited knowledge of French. The memo draws its power from a series of spare sentences, one after another, most sharing the same grammatical pattern, all but the last starting with a first-person pronoun.

I do not see how he can be effective in Laos without knowledge of the language. I would think that the Army must have many officers who have language facility. I would like to receive a report on whether attachés are expected to have a language facility in French or Spanish before they are sent to countries where these languages are spoken. I do not think we should expect an attaché to pick up the language upon his arrival there. Would you let me have your thoughts on this.

The president doesn't say he's annoyed, miffed, perplexed, or that 15 he never wants this to happen again. He doesn't need to, because his disapproval is conveyed by the grammar. The structure is austere; the language is plain; the message is clear. The last sentence, "Would you let me have your thoughts on this," translates to "Please make sure this never happens again."

Obviously, this tone is appropriate for a subordinate and not a peer. But even presidents have peers. When Kennedy wrote to Soviet premier Nikita Khrushchev on the subject of space travel, his grammar turned expansive, complex, almost lyrical.

Beyond these specific projects we are prepared now to discuss broader cooperation in the still more challenging projects which must be undertaken in the exploration of outer space. The tasks are so challenging, the costs so great, and the risks to the brave men who engage in space exploration so grave, that we must in all good conscience try every possibility of sharing these tasks and costs and of minimizing the risks.

In both cases, Kennedy knew who he wanted to be in relation to the person to whom he was writing—peeved boss to McNamara, visionary partner to fellow world leader Khrushchev.

But what if one of your peers gets out of line? Look at this letter from Kennedy to Khrushchev during the Cuban missile crisis, which echoes the note to McNamara in both structure and tone.

I have taken careful note of your statement that the events in Cuba might affect peace in all parts of the world. I trust that this does not mean that the Soviet government, using the situation in Cuba as a pretext, is planning to inflame other areas of the world. I would like to think that your government has too great a sense of responsibility to embark upon any enterprise so dangerous to general peace. . . . I believe, Mr. Chairman, that you should recognize that free peoples in all parts of the world do not accept the claim of historical inevitability for Communist revolution.

The Kennedy letters illustrate two surefire grammar guidelines, ones we'd all do well to keep in mind every time we dash off an email that's more than a sentence long:

1. Simple, short, repetitive grammar intensifies.
2. Complex, clause-filled, rhythmically varied sentences generally soften the message.

PUNCTUATION

It's OK to be lax so long as you're on email and on familiar terms with   20
the person to whom you're writing. With handhelds and IMing, the
rules are even looser.

It's useful to remind ourselves that punctuation originated as a reading tool. It was developed at a time when anyone who could write wrote by hand. Punctuation was a lifeline in a sea of poor handwriting and ink blotches. But email is completely legible. Generally, you can understand what someone is trying to tell you—even if periods and commas are dropped and paragraphs are littered with dashes.

Still, relaxed punctuation can do damage in a way that heedless uppercasing and lowercasing cannot. Punctuation is in some measure governed by your relationship to the person you're writing. If it's someone senior to you, punctuate correctly. If the email you received was properly punctuated, your correspondent deserves the same. This is something that's easy to forget. The speed, fluidity, and back-and-forth of email make it easier for all sorts of punctuation tics to creep into our writing. Witness, for example, the (confounding) growth in the use of trailing punctuation. "See you next summer . . ." or "We can just discuss this in the meeting . . ."

or "I lost my balloon . . ." We realize that email is often an ongoing conversation, but what's so bad about a period?

And note: any kind of relaxed punctuation is not appropriate in letters or memos. Also, keep in mind that even in email, if you drop, for example, an important comma, you can change the meaning of a sentence 180 degrees.

THE DANGERS OF MISSING PUNCTUATION

A friend of ours worked in an office where an email flame war erupted over a missing period. The email in question read:

No thanks to you.

It was supposed to say:

No. Thanks to you.

PARAGRAPHS

Keep them short.

Otherwise, people won't be able to read your emails easily on a computer screen.

Make sure you break a paragraph when you shift topics.

The key point or instruction should never be buried in a long paragraph.

Don't fear white space.

CONTRACTIONS

Our language comes with an option for paring the fat out of a sentence: contractions. But many people who constantly use contractions in speech will avoid them in writing. The colleague who says, "I don't know whether to get a cappuccino or a latte today," will minutes later write an email stating, "I do not know whether we should send the shipment today or tomorrow." The tone of the latter is more formal and can strike the ear as awkward or fussy; in addition, because it places more emphasis on the "not," it sounds more severe. Email—flat, informal, democratic email—should encourage us to use contractions in a way we'd never use them in formal letters.

In email, *not* contracting comes with a risk. As with so much else, it 30 all goes back to childhood. Parents tend to avoid contractions when teaching small children a lesson. "Do NOT put your fingers in the soup bowl, Elliott (or Ben or Natalie or Sophie); I am telling you that for the last time and I am NOT going to tell you again." The word "don't" is a warning; the phrase "do not" is both a warning and a reprimand. The uncontracted form puts the reader in young Elliott's place, and makes him feel as if he's being lectured by an authority figure. This can be useful when the warning you are giving is dire: the directive "Do not let the nuclear reactor overheat" is strengthened by the use of the freestanding "not." But "Do not make extra copies of the report" would probably be better served by a "don't," unless you mean to suggest that there will be dire consequences for doing so.

And this point isn't confined to contractions of the word "not." Many noncontractions manage to make the recipient feel scolded. The person who says, "I am upset," is probably more upset than the one who says, "I'm upset." In most general email correspondence, the contraction should be the default, the uncontracted form used for special emphasis.

CAPITALS

When words are written in CAPITAL LETTERS, it means that THE WRITER IS SHOUTING AT YOU. Since no one likes to be yelled at, and people generally shout when they feel that they can win only by intimidation and not by reason, it's a good rule never to compose entire emails in capitals, even cheery ones. For one thing, they're just that much harder to read because we aren't used to reading large blocks of capitalized text. And rarely is it a good idea to capitalize pejorative words—IDIOT, for example. These words are that much harsher when capitalized.

(You can, however, shout a word or two in joy or celebration. HOORAY is a word that is appropriately capitalized. It's a loud word that no one minds hearing louder. Ditto for CONGRATULATIONS and BON APPETIT.)

If you really want to aggravate someone, using all caps is an effective way to do it. A study of email users in the United States and Britain found that overuse of capitals was the thing that most irritated email recipients. (Emails that conveyed an overly friendly tone also made the most-annoying list, but only in the United Kingdom.)

Oddly, writing only in lowercase doesn't indicate the opposite of shouting—no one thinks you are whispering when you abstain from using capital letters. They just think you are too lazy to hit the Shift key from time to time. As with typos and abbreviations, people are more forgiving of this when they know you are sending them a message from a mobile device than when you are clearly at a desktop. There is, however, an implied casualness to all-lowercase communication. Generally, it's acceptable from an employer to an employee but not the other way around, among friends or colleagues, and especially in very short replies. But it's industry-specific—at many companies it's more the rule than the exception. When in doubt, though, capitalize normally, especially if someone wrote to you that way.

EMOTICONS

Even though we're well out of junior high, we like emoticons and think there are good uses for them. Pictographic smiling faces and those created out of punctuation marks—☺ and :)—bug many people but they make us smile. (So, of course, does sunshine on our shoulders.) Emoticons are an attempt to put a human face on faceless, quick communication. We also love the whole emoticon family, though we must admit that some of the more baroque manifestations can leave us perplexed—by what they are supposed to be and by when we'd use them. For example, =) :–)= is Abraham Lincoln and :OI is mouth full.

Emoticons are handy for the following:

1. They're great for text and instant messages and rapid-fire emails because they're really just a kind of shorthand.

2. They're helpful if you want to be cute, ironic, or tongue-in-cheek when writing those with whom you've already established a comfortable electronic correspondence. Certainly, you can use them with others who have used them with you.

However, emoticons should never be deployed when:

1. You're writing any kind of formal email or electronic message.

2. You're trying to compensate for a barb, a risky joke, or a sarcastic comment; the addition of an emoticon doesn't guarantee that there won't be hurt feelings.

* * *

ABBREVIATIONS

Abbreviations are like emoticons. They have an important function. FWIW (for what it's worth), PCM (please call me), W8 (wait)—all these facilitate communication, and in some cases they either help to bond people together in a shared language or are simply taken for granted. Whether an abbreviation seems silly or outlandish depends on where you sit. After all, is LOL, which some people sneer at, really inherently more opaque than FYI?

Of course, when the conversation is formal or you're not sure the other person knows the code, spell words out. 40

* * *

STUDY QUESTIONS

1. The authors list a number of elements that comprise a "perfect" e-mail. Which do you think are the most important? The least important? Why? They also list a number of e-mail hazards. Which are the worst? Why?

2. Consider this selection as a piece of advice. Evaluate its TONE, as well as the quality and quantity of examples provided. Are they effective? Are you likely to follow these authors' advice? Why or why not?

3. *For Writing.* Review a week's worth of e-mails that you have sent to your friends, instructors, and family. In an essay, ANALYZE your writing STYLE in each kind of e-mail. Do you see any kinds of patterns? How do you write differently for your different AUDIENCES? Does this analysis make you reconsider the way you write e-mail?

AMY TAN { *Mother Tongue*

AMY TAN (b.1952), the daughter of parents who emigrated from China, grew up in Oakland, California. In defiance of her mother's plan for her to pursue a career in medicine, Tan chose to study linguistics and pursue a career writing fiction. Tan's relationship with her mother figures prominently in her work, most notably in *The Joy Luck Club* (1989), her first and best-selling novel. The mother/daughter relationship is also central to "Mother Tongue," which first appeared in *Threepenny Review*. Tan's other works include *The Kitchen God's Wife* (1991), *The Bonesetter's Daughter* (2001), and *The Opposite of Fate* (2003).

In "Mother Tongue," Tan explores the different kinds of English she speaks and understands, taking into consideration her mother's English, the results of her own English achievement tests, and the reasons we don't see more Asian American writers. A remarkable ear for dialogue plays an important role in all of Tan's writing, and "Mother Tongue" is no exception. Notice how she weaves storytelling and dialogue, not only to inform and persuade, but also, through carefully crafted anecdotes, to help us understand her mother.

I AM NOT A SCHOLAR of English or literature. I cannot give you much more than personal opinions on the English language and its variations in this country or others.

I am a writer. And by that definition, I am someone who has always loved language. I am fascinated by language in daily life. I spend a great deal of my time thinking about the power of language—the way it can evoke an emotion, a visual image, a complex idea, or a simple truth. Language is the tool of my trade. And I use them all—all the Englishes I grew up with.

Recently, I was made keenly aware of the different Englishes I do use. I was giving a talk to a large group of people, the same talk I had already given to half a dozen other groups. The talk was about my writing, my life, and my book *The Joy Luck Club,* and it was going along well enough, until I remembered one major difference that made the whole talk sound wrong. My mother was in the room. And it was perhaps the first time she had heard me give a lengthy speech, using the kind of English I have never used with her. I was saying things like "the intersection of memory and imagination" and "There is an aspect of my fiction that relates to thus-and-thus"—a speech filled with carefully wrought grammatical phrases, burdened, it suddenly seemed to me, with nominalized forms, past perfect tenses, conditional phrases, forms of standard English that I had learned in school and through books, the forms of English I did not use at home with my mother.

Just last week, as I was walking down the street with her, I again found myself conscious of the English I was using, the English I do use with her. We were talking about the price of new and used furniture, and I heard myself saying this: "Not waste money that way." My husband was with us as well, and he didn't notice any switch in my English. And then I realized why. It's because over the twenty years we've been together I've often used the same kind of English with him, and sometimes he even uses it with me. It has become our language of intimacy, a different sort of English that relates to family talk, the language I grew up with.

So that you'll have some idea of what this family talk sounds like, I'll quote what my mother said during a conversation that I videotaped and then transcribed. During this conversation, she was talking about a political gangster in Shanghai who had the same last name as her family's, Du, and how in his early years the gangster wanted to be adopted by her family, who were rich by comparison. Later, the gangster became more powerful, far richer than my mother's family, and he showed up at my mother's wedding to pay his respects. Here's what she said in part:

"Du Yusong having business like fruit stand. Like off-the-street kind. He is Du like Du Zong—but not Tsung-ming Island people. The local people call *putong*. The river east side, he belong to that side local people. That man want to ask Du Zong father take him in like become own family. Du Zong father wasn't look down on him, but didn't take seriously, until that man big like become a mafia. Now important person, very hard to inviting him. Chinese way, came only to show respect, don't stay for dinner. Respect for making big celebration, he shows up. Mean gives lots of respect. Chinese custom. Chinese social life that way. If too important won't have to stay too long. He come to my wedding. I didn't see, I heard it. I gone to boy's side, they have YMCA dinner. Chinese age I was nineteen."

You should know that my mother's expressive command of English belies how much she actually understands. She reads the *Forbes* report, listens to *Wall Street Week,* converses daily with her stockbroker, reads Shirley MacLaine's books with ease—all kinds of things I can't begin to understand. Yet some of my friends tell me they understand fifty percent of what my mother says. Some say they understand eighty to ninety percent. Some say they understand none of it, as if she were speaking pure Chinese. But to me, my mother's English is perfectly clear, perfectly natural. It's my mother tongue. Her language, as I hear it, is vivid, direct, full of observation and imagery. That was the language that helped shape the way I saw things, expressed things, made sense of the world.

Lately I've been giving more thought to the kind of English my mother speaks. Like others, I have described it to people as "broken" or "fractured" English. But I wince when I say that. It has always bothered me that I can think of no way to describe it other than "broken," as if it were damaged and needed to be fixed, as if it lacked a certain wholeness and soundness. I've heard other terms used, "limited English," for example. But they seem just as bad, as if everything is limited, including people's perceptions of the limited-English speaker.

I know this for a fact, because when I was growing up, my mother's "limited" English limited my perception of her. I was ashamed of her English. I believed that her English reflected the quality of what she had to say. That is, because she expressed them imperfectly, her thoughts were imperfect. And I had plenty of empirical evidence to support me: the fact that people in department stores, at banks, and in restaurants did not take her seriously, did not give her good service, pretended not to understand her, or even acted as if they did not hear her.

My mother has long realized the limitations of her English as well. When I was a teenager, she used to have me call people on the phone and pretend I was she. In this guise, I was forced to ask for information or even to complain and yell at people who had been rude to her. One time it was a call to her stockbroker in New York. She had cashed out her small portfolio, and it just so happened we were going to New York the next week, our first trip outside California. I had to get on the phone and say in an adolescent voice that was not very convincing, "This is Mrs. Tan."

My mother was standing in the back whispering loudly, "Why he   10
don't send me check, already two weeks late. So mad he lie to me, losing me money."

And then I said in perfect English on the phone, "Yes, I'm getting rather concerned. You had agreed to send the check two weeks ago, but it hasn't arrived."

Then she began to talk more loudly. "What he want, I come to New York tell him front of his boss, you cheating me?" And I was trying to calm her down, make her be quiet, while telling the stockbroker, "I can't tolerate any more excuses. If I don't receive the check immediately, I am going to have to speak to your manager when I'm in New York next week." And sure enough, the following week, there we were in front of this astonished stockbroker, and I was sitting there red-faced and quiet, and my mother, the real Mrs. Tan, was shouting at his boss in her impeccable broken English.

We used a similar routine more recently, for a situation that was far less humorous. My mother had gone to the hospital for an appointment to find out about a CAT scan she had had a month earlier. She said she had spoken very good English, her best English, no mistakes. Still, she said, the hospital staff did not apologize when they informed her they had lost the CAT scan and she had come for othing. She said they did not seem to have any sympathy when she told them she was anxious to know the exact diagnosis, since both her husband and her son had died of brain tumors. She said they would not give her any more information until the next time and she would have to make another appointment for that. So she said she would not leave until the doctor called her daughter. She wouldn't budge. And when the doctor finally called her daughter, me, who spoke in perfect English—lo and behold—we had assurances the CAT scan would be found, promises that a conference call on Monday would be held, and apologies for any suffering my mother had gone through for a most regrettable mistake.

I think my mother's English almost had an effect on limiting my possibilities in life as well. Sociologists and linguists probably will tell you that a person's developing language skills are more influenced by peers than by family. But I do think that the language spoken in the family, especially in immigrant families which are more insular, plays a large role in shaping the language of the child. And I believe that it affected my results on achievement tests, IQ tests, and the SAT. While my English skills were never judged poor, compared with math, English could not be considered my strong suit. In grade school I did moderately well, getting perhaps B's, sometimes B-pluses, in English and scoring perhaps in the sixtieth or seventieth percentile on achievement tests. But those scores were not good enough to override the opinion that my true abilities lay in math and science, because in those areas I achieved A's and scored in the ninetieth percentile or higher.

This was understandable. Math is precise; there is only one correct 15 answer. Whereas, for me at least, the answers on English tests were always a judgment call, a matter of opinion and personal experience. Those tests were constructed around items like fill-in-the-blank sentence completion, such as "Even though Tom was _____ Mary thought he was _____." And the correct answer always seemed to be the most bland combinations, for example, "Even though Tom was shy, Mary thought he was charming," with the grammatical structure "even though" limiting the correct answer to some sort of semantic opposites, so you wouldn't get answers like "Even though Tom was foolish, Mary thought he was ridiculous." Well, according to my mother, there were very few limitations as to what Tom could have been and what Mary might have thought of him. So I never did well on tests like that.

The same was true with word analogies, pairs of words for which you were supposed to find some logical semantic relationship, for instance, "Sunset is to nightfall as _____ is to _____." And here you would be presented with a list of four possible pairs, one of which showed the same kind of relationship: *red* is to *stoplight, bus* is to *arrival, chills* is to *fever, yawn* is to *boring.* Well, I could never think that way. I knew what the tests were asking, but I could not block out of my mind the images already created by the first pair, *sunset* is to *nightfall*—and I would see a burst of colors against a darkening sky, the moon rising, the lowering of a curtain of stars. And all the other pairs of words—*red, bus, stoplight, boring*—just threw up a mass of confusing images, making it impossible for me to see that saying "A sunset precedes nightfall" was as logical as saying "A chill precedes a fever." The only way I would have gotten that answer right was to imagine an associative situation, such as my being disobedient and staying out past sunset, catching a chill at night, which turned into feverish pneumonia as punishment—which indeed did happen to me.

I have been thinking about all this lately, about my mother's English, about achievement tests. Because lately I've been asked, as a writer, why there are not more Asian-Americans represented in American literature. Why are there few Asian-Americans enrolled in creative writing programs? Why do so many Chinese students go into engineering? Well, these are broad sociological questions I can't begin to answer. But I have noticed in surveys—in fact, just last week—that Asian-American students, as a whole, do significantly better on math achievement tests than on English tests. And this makes me think that there are other Asian-American students whose English spoken in the home might also be described as "broken" or "limited." And perhaps they also have teachers who are steering them away from writing and into math and science, which is what happened to me.

Fortunately, I happen to be rebellious and enjoy the challenge of disproving assumptions made about me. I became an English major my first year in college, after being enrolled as pre-med. I started writing nonfiction as a freelancer the week after I was told by my boss at the time that writing was my worst skill and I should hone my talents toward account management.

But it wasn't until 1985 that I began to write fiction. At first I wrote what I thought to be wittily crafted sentences, sentences that would finally prove I had mastery over the English language. Here's an example from the first draft of a story that later made its way into *The Joy Luck Club,* but without this line: "That was my mental quandary in its nascent state." A terrible line, which I can barely pronounce.

Fortunately, for reasons I won't get into here, I later decided I 20 should envision a reader for the stories I would write. And the reader I decided on was my mother, because these were stories about mothers. So with this reader in mind—and in fact she did read my early drafts—I began to write stories using all the Englishes I grew up with: the English I spoke to my mother, which for lack of a better term might be described as "simple"; the English she used with me, which for lack of a better term might be described as "broken"; my translation of her Chinese, which could certainly be described as "watered down"; and what I imagined to be her translation of her Chinese if she could speak in perfect English, her internal language, and for that I sought to preserve the essence, but neither an English nor a Chinese structure. I wanted to capture what language ability tests could never reveal: her intent, her passion, her imagery, the rhythms of her speech and the nature of her thoughts.

Apart from what any critic had to say about my writing, I knew I had succeeded where it counted when my mother finished reading my book and gave me her verdict: "So easy to read."

STUDY QUESTIONS

1. Explain the pun in the title of Tan's essay.

2. Identify the different "Englishes" Tan discusses. What does she want her reader to understand about these different dialects?

3. Tan writes, "Fortunately, for reasons I won't get into here, I later decided I should envision a reader for the stories I would write. And the reader I decided on was my mother, because these were stories about mothers." How might the mental picture of her mother reading her stories have affected Tan's VOICE? When writing for college, whom do you most often envision as your reader? How does this affect the decisions you make in your writing?

4. *For Writing.* Write an essay DESCRIBING your own "Englishes." Even if English is your only language, it's likely that you speak differently with different people—using with some, for instance, more formal language than with others. Think of how you talk with friends, parents, grandparents, children, siblings, and professors. How does your DICTION and syntax vary with different people? Do you have a special "English" for a particular MEDIUM, such as text-messaging or letter-writing? Describe at least three different ways you use language for different AUDIENCES and mediums and explain why you talk or write the way you do in each instance.

DEBORAH TANNEN

{ *Sex, Lies and Conversation:*
Why Is It So Hard for Men and
Women to Talk to Each Other?

DEBORAH TANNEN (b. 1945) earned a PhD in linguistics at the
University of California, Berkeley, in 1979 and is a professor of linguistics
at Georgetown University. She is best known for her research on how
people of different genders attempt to communicate with each other.
Tannen has published more than one hundred articles in scholarly journals
as well as most major American magazines and newspapers; she has written
more than twenty books, including *You Just Don't Understand: Women
and Men in Conversation* (1990), which spent nearly four years on the
New York Times best-seller list and has been translated into twenty-nine
languages. Other books include *You're Wearing That? Understanding
Mothers and Daughters in Conversation* (2006) and *You Were Always Mom's
Favorite: Sisters in Conversation Throughtout Their Lives* (2009). A frequent guest on radio and television programs, she has appeared on NPR's
Morning Edition, *20/20*, *Good Morning America*, *Oprah*, and *The Colbert
Report*, among others.

The following article, which appeared in the *Washington Post* in
1990, offers an encapsulated version of Tannen's research on how men
and women speak with each other. Tannen compares and contrasts conversational styles and offers plenty of examples to demonstrate how different
expectations and understandings of conversational cues affect how men
and women communicate with each other. The next time you speak with a
member of the opposite sex, it might help you to understand that your communication is truly, as Tannen calls it, "cross-cultural." As you read, notice
the kinds of evidence Tannen supplies to support her ideas.

I WAS ADDRESSING A SMALL gathering in a suburban Virginia living room—a women's group that had invited men to join them. Throughout the evening, one man had been particularly talkative, frequently offering ideas and anecdotes, while his wife sat silently beside him on the couch. Toward the end of the evening, I commented that women frequently complain that their husbands don't talk to them. This man quickly concurred. He gestured toward his wife and said, "She's the talker in our family." The room burst into laughter; the man looked puzzled and hurt. "It's true," he explained. "When I come home from work I have nothing to say. If she didn't keep the conversation going, we'd spend the whole evening in silence."

This episode crystallizes the irony that although American men tend to talk more than women in public situations, they often talk less at home. And this pattern is wreaking havoc with marriage.

The pattern was observed by political scientist Andrew Hacker in the late '70s. Sociologist Catherine Kohler Riessman reports in her new book *Divorce Talk* that most of the women she interviewed—but only a few of the men—gave lack of communication as the reason for their divorces. Given the current divorce rate of nearly 50 percent, that amounts to millions of cases in the United States every year—a virtual epidemic of failed conversation.

In my own research, complaints from women about their husbands most often focused not on tangible inequities such as having given up the chance for a career to accompany a husband to his, or doing far more than their share of daily life-support work like cleaning, cooking, social arrangements and errands. Instead, they focused on communication: "He doesn't listen to me," "He doesn't talk to me," I found, as Hacker observed years before, that most wives want their husbands to be, first and foremost, conversational partners, but few husbands share this expectation of their wives.

In short, the image that best represents the current crisis is the 5 stereotypical cartoon scene of a man sitting at the breakfast table with a newspaper held up in front of his face, while a woman glares at the back of it, wanting to talk.

LINGUISTIC BATTLE OF THE SEXES

How can women and men have such different impressions of communication in marriage? Why the widespread imbalance in their interests and expectations?

In the April issue of *American Psychologist,* Stanford University's Eleanor Maccoby reports the results of her own and others' research showing that children's development is most influenced by the social structure of peer interactions. Boys and girls tend to play with children of their own gender, and their sex-separate groups have different organizational structures and interactive norms.

I believe these systematic differences in childhood socialization make talk between women and men like cross-cultural communication, heir to all the attraction and pitfalls of that enticing but difficult enterprise. My research on men's and women's conversations uncovered patterns similar to those described for children's groups.

For women, as for girls, intimacy is the fabric of relationships, and talk is the thread from which it is woven. Little girls create and maintain friendships by exchanging secrets; similarly, women regard conversation as the cornerstone of friendship. So a woman expects her husband to be a new and improved version of a best friend. What is important is not the individual subjects that are discussed but the sense of closeness, of a life shared, that emerges when people tell their thoughts, feelings, and impressions.

Bonds between boys can be as intense as girls', but they are based   10
less on talking, more on doing things together. Since they don't assume talk is the cement that binds a relationship, men don't know what kind of talk women want, and they don't miss it when it isn't there.

Boys' groups are larger, more inclusive, and more hierarchical, so boys must struggle to avoid the subordinate position in the group. This may play a role in women's complaints that men don't listen to them. Some men really don't like to listen, because being the listener makes them feel one-down, like a child listening to adults or an employee to a boss.

But often when women tell men, "You aren't listening," and the men protest, "I am," the men are right. The impression of not listening results from misalignments in the mechanics of conversation. The misalignment begins as soon as a man and a woman take physical positions. This became clear when I studied videotapes made by psychologist Bruce Dorval of children and adults talking to their same-sex best friends. I found that at every age, the girls and women faced each other directly, their eyes anchored on each other's faces. At every age, the boys and men sat at angles to each other and looked elsewhere in the room, periodically glancing at each other. They were obviously attuned to each other, often mirroring each other's movements. But the tendency of men to face away can give women the impression they aren't listening even when they are. A young woman in college was frustrated: Whenever she told her boyfriend she wanted to talk to him, he would lie down on the floor, close his eyes, and put his arm over his face. This signaled to her, "He's taking a nap." But he insisted he was listening extra hard. Normally, he looks around the room, so he is easily distracted. Lying down and covering his eyes helped him concentrate on what she was saying.

Analogous to the physical alignment that women and men take in conversation is their topical alignment. The girls in my study tended to talk at length about one topic, but the boys tended to jump from topic to topic. The second-grade girls exchanged stories about people they knew. The second-grade boys teased, told jokes, noticed things in the room and talked about finding games to play. The sixth-grade girls talked about problems with a mutual friend. The sixth grade boys talked about fifty-five different topics, none of which extended over more than a few turns.

LISTENING TO BODY LANGUAGE

Switching topics is another habit that gives women the impression men aren't listening, especially if they switch to a topic about themselves. But the evidence of the tenth-grade boys in my study indicates otherwise. The tenth-grade boys sprawled across their chairs with bodies parallel and eyes straight ahead, rarely looking at each other. They looked as if they were riding in a car, staring out the windshield. But they were talking about their feelings. One boy was upset because a girl had told him he had a drinking problem, and the other was feeling alienated from all his friends.

Now, when a girl told a friend about a problem, the friend 15 responded by asking probing questions and expressing agreement and understanding. But the boys dismissed each other's problems. Todd assured Richard that his drinking was "no big problem" because "sometimes you're funny when you're off your butt." And when Todd said he felt left out, Richard responded, "Why should you? You know more people than me."

Women perceive such responses as belittling and unsupportive. But the boys seemed satisfied with them. Whereas women reassure each other by implying, "You shouldn't feel bad because I've had similar experiences," men do so by implying, "You shouldn't feel bad because your problems aren't so bad."

There are even simpler reasons for women's impression that men don't listen. Linguist Lynette Hirschman found that women make more listener-noise, such as "mhm," "uhuh," and "yeah," to show "I'm with you." Men, she found, more often give silent attention. Women who expect a stream of listener noise interpret silent attention as no attention at all.

Women's conversational habits are as frustrating to men as men's are to women. Men who expect silent attention interpret a stream of listener noise as overreaction or impatience. Also, when women talk to each other in a close, comfortable setting, they often overlap, finish each other's sentences and anticipate what the other is about to say. This practice, which I call "participatory listenership," is often perceived by men as interruption, intrusion and lack of attention.

A parallel difference caused a man to complain about his wife, "She just wants to talk about her own point of view. If I show her another view, she gets mad at me." When most women talk to each other, they assume a conversationalist's job is to express agreement and support. But many men see their conversational duty as pointing out the other side of an argument. This is heard as disloyalty by women, and refusal to offer the requisite support. It is not that women don't want to see other points of view, but that they prefer them phrased as suggestions and inquiries rather than as direct challenges.

In his book *Fighting for Life,* Walter Ong points out that men   20
use "agonistic," or warlike, oppositional formats to do almost anything; thus discussion becomes debate, and conversation a competitive
sport. In contrast, women see conversation as a ritual means of establishing rapport. If Jane tells a problem and June says she has a similar
one, they walk away feeling closer to each other. But this attempt at
establishing rapport can backfire when used with men. Men take too
literally women's ritual "troubles talk," just as women mistake men's
ritual challenges for real attack.

THE SOUNDS OF SILENCE

These differences begin to clarify why women and men have such different expectations about communication in marriage. For women, talk
creates intimacy. Marriage is an orgy of closeness: you can tell your
feelings and thoughts, and still be loved. Their greatest fear is being
pushed away. But men live in a hierarchical world, where talk main-
tains independence and status. They are on guard to protect themselves from being put down and pushed around.

This explains the paradox of the talkative man who said of his silent
wife, "She's the talker." In the public setting of a guest lecture, he felt
challenged to show his intelligence and display his understanding of
the lecture. But at home, where he has nothing to prove and no one to
defend against, he is free to remain silent. For his wife, being home
means she is free from the worry that something she says might offend
someone, or spark disagreement, or appear to be showing off; at home
she is free to talk.

The communication problems that endanger marriage can't be
fixed by mechanical engineering. They require a new conceptual
framework about the role of talk in human relationships. Many of the
psychological explanations that have become second nature may not
be helpful, because they tend to blame either women (for not being
assertive enough) or men (for not being in touch with their feelings). A
sociolinguistic approach by which male-female conversation is seen as
cross-cultural communication allows us to understand the problem
and forge solutions without blaming either party.

Once the problem is understood, improvement comes naturally, as it did to the young woman and her boyfriend who seemed to go to sleep when she wanted to talk. Previously, she had accused him of not listening, and he had refused to change his behavior, since that would be admitting fault. But then she learned about and explained to him the differences in women's and men's habitual ways of aligning themselves in conversation. The next time she told him she wanted to talk, he began, as usual, by lying down and covering his eyes. When the familiar negative reaction bubbled up, she reassured herself that he really was listening. But then he sat up and looked at her. Thrilled, she asked why. He said, "You like me to look at you when we talk, so I'll try to do it." Once he saw their differences as cross-cultural rather than right and wrong, he independently altered his behavior.

Women who feel abandoned and deprived when their husbands 25 won't listen to or report daily news may be happy to discover their husbands trying to adapt once they understand the place of small talk in women's relationships. But if their husbands don't adapt, the women may still be comforted that for men, this is not a failure of intimacy. Accepting the difference, the wives may look to their friends or family for that kind of talk. And husbands who can't provide it shouldn't feel their wives have made unreasonable demands. Some couples will still decide to divorce, but at least their decisions will be based on realistic expectations.

In these times of resurgent ethnic conflicts, the world desperately needs cross-cultural understanding. Like charity, successful cross-cultural communication should begin at home.

STUDY QUESTIONS

1. According to Tannen, what conversational cues tell women someone is listening closely? What conversational cues tell men they're being listened to? How do women express support in conversation? How do men?

2. Tannen COMPARES AND CONTRASTS men's and women's conversational strategies in same-gender groups in order to determine how they might speak more effectively with each other. On what points does she compare them? (For instance, one point of comparison is the use of "listener noise.") What other points of comparison might she have examined?

4. What is Tannen's CLAIM? What REASONS does she supply to support that claim? What kinds of EVIDENCE does she supply? How effective are they?

5. *For Writing.* Seek out two sustained conversations: first with someone of the opposite gender, and then with someone of your own gender. Do you notice any of the conversational strategies Tannen mentions? Write an essay in which you ANALYZE the conversations in terms of male and female conversational styles, and apply Tannen's generalizations about male and female approaches to them. Does what you observed match her conclusions?

FRANCINE WEINBERG

RICHARD BULLOCK

W. W. NORTON

{ *Glossary*

ABSTRACT A genre of writing that summarizes a book, an article, or a paper, usually in 100–200 words. Authors in some academic fields must provide, at the top of a report submitted for publication, an abstract of its content. The abstract may then appear in a journal of abstracts, such as *Psychological Abstracts*. An *informative abstract* summarizes a complete report; a briefer *descriptive abstract* works more as a teaser; a stand-alone *proposal abstract* (also called a **topic proposal**) requests permission to conduct research, write on a topic, or present a report at a scholarly conference. Key Features: **summary** of basic information • objective description • brevity.

ACTION VERB A **verb** that expresses a physical or mental action (*jump, consider*).

ACTIVE VOICE A grammatical construction in which the subject or agent of the action is also its grammatical subject: *The boy hit the baseball. See also* **passive voice.**

AD HOMINEM **ARGUMENT** A logical fallacy that attacks someone's character rather than addressing the issues.

ADJECTIVE A **modifier** that describes a **noun** or **pronoun** (*a challenging task, a cloudless blue sky*).

ADVERB A **modifier** that tells more about a **verb** (*speak loudly*), an **adjective** (*extremely loud*), another adverb (*very loudly*), or a whole **clause** (*Sometimes you need to speak loudly*).

ALLEGORY An extended **metaphor**, in which one thing (usually nonrational, abstract, religious) is implicitly spoken of in terms of something concrete. In an allegory, the comparison is expressed in an entire work or large portion of a work.

ANALYSIS A genre of writing that methodically examines a topic or text by breaking it into its parts and noting how they work in relation to one another.

ANECDOTES Brief **narratives** used to illustrate a point.

ANNOTATED BIBLIOGRAPHY A genre of writing that gives an overview of the published research and scholarship on a topic. Each entry includes complete publication information and a **summary** or an **abstract** for each source. A *descriptive annotation* summarizes the content of a source without commenting on its value; an *evaluative annotation* gives an opinion about the source along with a description of it. Key Features: statement of the scope • complete bibliographic information • relevant commentary • consistent presentation.

APA STYLE A system of documenting sources used in the social sciences. APA stands for the American Psychological Association. *See also* **documentation.**

APPENDIX A section at the end of a written work for supplementary material that would be distracting in the main part of the text.

APPLICATION LETTERS Letters written to apply for jobs or other opportunities. *See also* résumés. Key Features: succinct indication of qualifications • reasonable and pleasing **tone** • conventional, businesslike form.

ARGUING A **strategy** that can be used in any kind of writing to support a **claim** with **reasons** and **evidence.**

ARGUMENT, ARGUMENTATIVE ESSAY A **genre** of writing that uses **reasons** and **evidence** to support a **claim** or position and, sometimes, to persuade an **audience** to accept that position.

Key Features: clear and arguable position • necessary background • good reasons • convincing support for each reason • appeal to readers' values • trustworthy **tone** • careful consideration of other positions.

ARTICLE The word *a, an,* or *the,* used to indicate that a **noun** is indefinite (*a, an*) or definite (*the*).

AUDIENCE Those to whom a text is directed—the people who read, listen to, or view the text. Audience is a key part of every text's **rhetorical situation.**

AUTHORITIES People or texts that are cited as support for a writer's **argument.** A structural engineer may be quoted as an authority on bridge construction, for example. *Authority* also refers to a quality conveyed by a writer who is knowledgeable about his or her subject.

BANDWAGON APPEAL A logical **fallacy** that argues for a thought or an action solely because others support it.

BEGGING THE QUESTION A logical **fallacy** that goes in a circle, assuming as a given what the writer is trying to prove.

BILDUNGSROMAN A novel that depicts the growth and development of a **character** and the character's self-understanding.

BLOCK QUOTATION In a written work, long **quotations** are set off indented and without quotation marks. In **MLA style**: set off text more than four typed lines, indented ten spaces (or one inch) from the left margin. In **APA style**: set off quotes of forty or more words, indented five spaces (or half an inch) from the left margin. *See also* **quotation.**

BLOG From *Web log*, a Web site with frequent postings by its authors, links to other sites, and comments posted by readers. Blogs present personal opinion and so should not be considered authoritative sources.

CAUSE AND EFFECT A **strategy** for analyzing why something occurred and/or what its consequences are. Sometimes cause and effect serves as the **organizing** principle for a whole text.

CBE STYLE A system of documenting sources in the sciences. CBE stands for the Council of Biology Editors. *See also* **documentation.**

CHARACTER (1) A fictional person who acts, appears, or is referred to in a work; (2) a combination of a person's qualities, especially moral qualities, so that such terms as "good" and "bad," "strong" and "weak," often apply.

CHARACTERIZATION The artistic presentation of a person in fiction or nonfiction. A term like "a good character" can, then, be ambiguous—it may mean that the character is virtuous or that he or she is well presented by the writer regardless of his or her characteristics or moral qualities.

CHRONOLOGICAL ORDER A way of organizing text that proceeds from the beginning of an event to the end. Reverse chronological order proceeds in the other direction, from the end to the beginning. *See also* **in medias res.**

CITATION In a text, the act of crediting information from a source. A citation and its corresponding parenthetical **documentation** or footnote or endnote provide minimal information about the source, and complete bibliographic information appears in a list of **works cited** or **references** at the end of the text.

CLAIM A statement that asserts a belief or position. In an **argument**, a claim needs to be stated in a **thesis** or clearly implied, and requires support with **reasons** and **evidence.**

CLASSIFY AND DIVIDE, CLASSIFICATION AND DIVISION A **strategy** that either groups (classifies) numerous individual items by their similarities (for example, classifying cereal, bread, butter, chicken, cheese, ice cream, eggs, and oil as carbohydrates, proteins, and fats) or breaks (divides) one large category into smaller categories (for example, dividing food into carbohydrates, proteins, and fats). Sometimes classification and/or division serves as the **organizing** principle for a whole text.

CLAUSE A group of words that consists of at least a **subject** and a **predicate**; a clause may be either **independent** or **subordinate**.

CLIMAX The point at which the action stops rising and begins falling or reversing.

CLUSTERING A process for **generating ideas and text**, in which a writer visually connects thoughts by jotting them down and drawing lines between related items.

COHERENCE The quality that allows an **audience** to follow a text's meaning and to *see* the connections among ideas, sentences, and paragraphs. Elements that can help to achieve coherence include the title, a clearly stated or implied **thesis**, **topic sentences**, an easy-to-follow organization with clear **transitions**, and parallelism among comparable ideas.

COLLABORATION The **process** of working with others.

COMMA SPLICE Two or more **independent clauses** joined by only a comma: *I live free, I love life.*

COMMON GROUND Shared values. Writers build common ground with **audiences** by acknowledging others' **points of view**, seeking areas of compromise, and using language that includes, rather than excludes, those they aim to reach.

COMPARE AND CONTRAST, COMPARISON AND CONTRAST A **strategy** that highlights the similarities and differences between items. Using the *block method* of comparison and contrast, a writer discusses all the points about one item and then all the same points about the next item; using the *point-by-point method*, a writer discusses one point for both items before going on to discuss the next point for both items, and so on. Sometimes comparison and/or contrast serves as the **organizing** principle for a whole text.

COMPLEMENT A **noun**, noun phrase, **pronoun**, or **adjective** that modifies either the **subject** or the direct **object** of a sentence. A subject complement follows a **linking verb** and tells more about the subject: *She is a good speaker. She is eloquent.* An object complement describes or renames the direct object: *Critics called the movie a masterpiece. We found the movie enjoyable.*

CONFLICT A struggle between opposing forces, such as between two people, between a person and something in nature or society, or even between two drives, impulses, or parts of the self.

CONVINCE, CONVINCING In **argument**, to present **evidence**, usually in the form of facts and figures, in support of the writer's opinion. Convincing may differ from **persuading** in that convincing is designed to get the reader to agree while persuading is designed to get the reader to act.

COUNTERARGUMENT In **argument**, an alternative **position** or objections to the writer's position. The writer of an argument should not only acknowledge counterarguments but also, if at all possible, accept, accommodate, or refute each counterargument.

CREDIBILITY The sense of trustworthiness that a writer conveys through his or her text.

CRITERIA In an **evaluation**, the standards against which something is judged.

CUBING A process for generating ideas and text in which a writer looks at a topic in six ways—to **describe** it, to **compare** it to something else, to associate it with other things or **classify** it, to analyze it (*see* **analysis**), to apply it, and to argue for or against it (*see* **argument**).

DEDUCTION, DEDUCTIVE REASONING In **argument**, a method of drawing a conclusion in which the writer asserts that a thing is true based on general or universal premises (moving from the general to the specific): *Every virtue is laudable; kindness is a virtue; therefore kindness is laudable.*

DEFINE, DEFINITION A strategy that gets at the meaning of something. Three main kinds of definitions are the *formal definition*, which may iden-

tify the category that something belongs to and tell what distinguishes it from other things in that category: for example, defining a worm as an invertebrate (a category) with a long, rounded body and no appendages (distinguishing features); the *extended definition*, which, as its name suggests is longer: for example, a paragraph explaining where a worm fits in the animal kingdom and what its closest relatives are; and the *stipulative definition*, which gives the writer's particular use of a term: for example, using the term *worm* to refer to a kind of gummy candy. Sometimes definition serves as the **organizing** principle for a whole text.

DÉNOUEMENT The final part of a **plot**, in which the action is resolved.

DESCRIBE, DESCRIPTION A **strategy** that tells how something looks, sounds, smells, feels, or tastes. Effective description creates a clear **dominant impression** built from specific details. Description can be *objective, subjective,* or both. Sometimes description serves as the **organizing** principle for a whole text.

DESIGN The way a text is arranged and presented visually. Elements of design include typeface, color, illustration, layout, and white space. One component of a **rhetorical situation**, design plays an important part in reaching a text's **audience** and achieving its **purpose**.

DIALOGUE A strategy of adding people's own words to a text. A writer often uses dialogue to add detail and interest.

DICTION A writer's choice of words, particularly with regard to clarity, correctness, and/or effectiveness in writing.

DISCOVERY DRAFTING A process of drafting something quickly, mostly for the purpose of discovering what one wants to say.

DIVIDE, DIVISION *See* **classify and divide.**

DOCUMENTATION Publication information about the sources cited in a text. The documentation usually appears in an abbreviated form in parentheses at the point of **citation** or in an endnote or a footnote. Complete documentation usually appears as a list of **works cited** or **references** at the end of the text. Documentation styles vary by discipline. For example, Modern Language Association (MLA) style requires the author's complete first name if it appears in a source, whereas American Psychological Association (APA) and the Council of Biology Editors (CBE) style requires only the initial of the author's first name.

DOCUMENTED ESSAY A genre of writing in which the writer cites information drawn from other sources. Key Features: use of **primary** and/or **secondary sources** • **analysis** or **interpretation** • documentation.

DOMINANT IMPRESSION The overall effect created through specific details when a writer **describes** something.

DOMINO THEORY The theory that if one event is allowed to take place, a series of similar events will follow, as when a line of dominoes is placed on end close together, toppling one will cause the entire line to fall.

DRAFTING The process of putting words on paper or screen. Writers often write several drafts, **revising** each until they achieve their goal or reach a deadline. At that point, they submit a finished final draft.

EDITING The process of fine-tuning a text—examining each word, phrase, sentence, and paragraph—to be sure that the text is correct and precise and says exactly what the writer intends. *See also* **proofreading** and **revising.**

EITHER-OR ARGUMENT A logical **fallacy** that oversimplifies to suggest that only two possible **positions** exist on a complex issue. The fallacy is also known as a **false dilemma.**

ETHNOGRAPHY A genre of writing that uses **fieldwork**—interviewing and observing—to present a picture of a group of people. Key Features: focus on members of a specific group • observation over time in group's natural setting • close analysis of a few members.

ETHOS A mode of persuasion that appeals to the character, feelings, moral nature, or guiding beliefs of a person, group, or institution; in writing, ethos can refer to the attempt by the writer or speaker to demonstrate his or her credibility.

EVALUATION A genre of writing that makes a judgment about something—a source, poem, film, restaurant, whatever—based on certain criteria. Key Features: description of the subject • clearly defined criteria • knowledgeable discussion of the subject • balanced and fair assessment.

EVIDENCE The data you present to support your reasons. Such data may include statistics, calculations, examples, anecdotes, quotations, case studies, or anything else that will convince your reader that your reasons are compelling. Evidence should be sufficient (enough to show that the reasons have merit) and relevant (appropriate to the argument you're making).

EXAMPLE, EXEMPLIFICATION A strategy that uses examples to clarify or support a point.

EXPLAINING A PROCESS *See* process analysis.

EXPLETIVE A word such as *it* or *there* that stands in for information provided later in the sentence: *It was difficult to drive on the icy road. There is plenty of food in the refrigerator.*

EXPOSITION, EXPOSITORY (1) In literature, the first part of a plot, where background information is established; (2) in composition and rhetoric, a rhetorical strategy whose main purpose is to inform the reader about a subject through explanation, interpretation, clarification, or other means.

FABLE A genre of writing that employs a typically legendary story with a lesson to be learned by its audience. Key Features: animal characters or personified natural forces • an instructive purpose • ends with a moral (a short, easily remembered lesson).

FALLACY, LOGICAL Faulty reasoning that can mislead an audience. Fallacies include *ad hominem*, bandwagon appeal, begging the question, either-or argument (also called false dilemma), false analogy, faulty causality (also called *post hoc, ergo propter hoc*), hasty generalization, and slippery slope.

FALLING ACTION the fourth part of action in a classical plot, during which the audience sees the effects of the conflict.

FALSE ANALOGY A fallacy comparing things that do resemble each other but that are not alike in the most important respects.

FALSE DILEMMA *See* either-or argument.

FAULTY CAUSALITY *See post hoc, ergo propter hoc.*

FIELD RESEARCH, FIELDWORK The collection of firsthand data through observation, interviews, and questionnaires or surveys.

FLASHBACK In narrative (*see* **narrate**), an interruption of the main story in order to show an incident that occurred at an earlier time.

FORMAL WRITING Writing intended to be evaluated by someone such as an instructor or read by an **audience** expecting academic or businesslike argument and presentation. Formal writing should be carefully **revised, edited,** and **proofread.** *See also* **informal writing.**

FRAGMENT, SENTENCE A group of words that is capitalized and punctuated as a sentence but is not one, either because it lacks a **subject,** a **verb,** or both, or because it begins with a word that makes it a **subordinate clause.**

FRAME STORY A story that surrounds another story, often used as an introductory device or **organizing** principle.

FREEWRITING A process for generating **ideas and text** by writing continuously for several minutes without pausing to read what has been written.

FUSED SENTENCE Two or more **independent clauses** with no punctuation between them: *I live free I love life.*

GENERATING IDEAS AND TEXT A set of processes, such as **freewriting,** clus-tering, and **looping,** that helps writers think of **topics, examples, reasons, evidence,** and other parts of a text.

GENRE A classification of text marked by and expected to have certain key features and to follow certain conventions of style and presentation. In the literary world, readers recognize such genres as the short story and novel (which are expected to have **plots**) and the poem (which may not have a plot but has other characteristics, such as rhythm); in academic and workplace settings, readers and writers focus on other genres, which also meet expectations in content, style, and appearance. Genres include **abstracts, annotated bibliographies, application letters, arguments, ethnographies, evaluations, lab reports, literacy narratives, literary analyses, profiles, proposals, reflections, résumés, reports,** and **textual analyses.**

HASTY GENERALIZATION A **fallacy** that reaches a conclusion based on insufficient or inappropriately qualified evidence.

HOME PAGE The introductory page of a Web site.

HYPERBOLE An over-the-top exaggeration: *I'll bet you a million bucks I'll get an A on my paper.*

IMAGERY Broadly defined, any sensory detail or evocation in a work; more nar-

153

rowly, the use of figurative language to evoke a feeling, to call to mind an idea, or to describe an object.

IN MEDIAS RES In the middle of things (Latin); a device for introducing a subject in the middle of the action, rather than at the chronological beginning.

INDEFINITE PRONOUN A pronoun, such as *all, anyone, anything, everyone, everything, few, many, some,* and *something,* that functions like a **noun** but does not refer to or take the place of a specific noun.

INDEPENDENT CLAUSE A **clause,** containing a **subject** and a **verb,** that can stand alone as a sentence: *She sang. The world-famous soprano sang several popular arias.*

INDUCTION, INDUCTIVE REASONING In **argument,** a method of drawing a conclusion in which the writer asserts that a thing is true by generalizing from a particular observation (moving from the specific to the general): *All the squirrels I have seen are brown; therefore all squirrels are brown.* Note that this particular observation can be proved wrong, since others have observed white and black squirrels.

INFORMAL WRITING Writing not intended to be evaluated—sometimes not even read—by others. Informal writing is produced primarily to explore ideas or to communicate casually with friends and acquaintances. *See also* **formal writing.**

INQUIRY, WRITING AS A process for investigating a topic by posing questions, searching for multiple answers, and keeping an open mind.

INTERPRETATION The act of making sense of something or explaining what one thinks it means. Interpretation is the goal of writing a **literary analysis** or **textual analysis.**

IRONY A situation or statement characterized by a significant difference between what is expected or understood and what actually happens or is meant.

JOURNALISTIC NARRATIVE A **genre** of writing that prizes accuracy, objectivity, and balance, telling a story in the most impartial and efficient way possible. Key Features: answers the questions *who, what, where, when, why,* and *how,* usually in the first paragraph • simple writing **style** • most important facts placed first, details filled in later • includes **quotations** from people involved.

KEYWORD A term that a researcher inputs when searching databases and online search engines for information.

LAB REPORT A **genre** of writing that covers the process of conducting an experiment in a controlled setting. Key Features: explicit title • **abstract** • statement of **purpose** • methods •

results and discussion • **references** • **appendix** • appropriate format.

LAYOUT The way text is arranged on a page or screen—for example, in paragraphs, in lists, on charts, and with headings.

LETTER WRITING A process of generating ideas and text by going through the motions of writing a letter to someone to explain a **topic.**

LINK On a Web page, a URL, word, or image that, when clicked, opens a different page.

LINKING VERB A verb that expresses a state of being (*appear, be, feel, seem*).

LISTING A process for generating ideas and text by making lists while thinking about a topic, finding relationships among the notes, and arranging the notes as an outline (*see* **outlining**).

LITERACY NARRATIVE A genre of writing that tells about a writer's experience learning to read or write, or about the role of literacy or knowledge in the writer's life. Key Features: well-told story • vivid detail • indication of the narrative's significance.

LITERACY PORTFOLIO An organized collection of materials showing examples of one writer's progress as a reader and/or writer.

LITERARY ANALYSIS A **genre** of writing that argues for a particular **interpretation** of a literary text—most often fiction, poetry, or drama. *See also* **analysis** and **textual analysis.** Key Features: arguable **thesis** • careful attention to the language of the text • attention to patterns or themes • clear interpretation • MLA style.

LITERATURE (1) Literary works, including fiction, poetry, drama, and some nonfiction; (2) the body of written work produced in given field.

LOGICAL FALLACY *See* **fallacy, logical.**

LOGOS A mode of **persuasion** that appeals to logic; that is, an attempt by the writer or speaker to prove a point through logical reasoning. *See also* **deduction** and **induction.**

LOOPING A process for generating ideas and text in which a writer writes about a topic quickly for several minutes and then summarizes the most important or interesting idea in a sentence, which becomes the beginning of another round of writing and summarizing. The process continues until the writer finds an angle for a paper.

MEDIUM (PL. MEDIA) A means for communicating—for example, in print, with speech, or online. Texts consisting of words are said to use *verbal media* (or oral/aural), whereas photographs, films, and sculptures are examples of *visual media* (though some verbal texts include visual images, and some visual texts include words).

MEMOIR A **genre** of writing that focuses on something significant from the writer's past. Key Features: good story • vivid details • clear significance.

METAPHOR A figure of speech that makes a comparison without using the word *like* or *as*: *"All the world's a stage /And all the men and women merely players"* (William Shakespeare, *As You Like It* 2.7.138–39).

MLA STYLE A system of documenting sources used in the humanities and fine arts. MLA stands for the Modern Language Association. *See also* **documentation.**

MODAL A helping **verb** such as *can, could, may, might, must, should, will,* or *would* that indicates probability or necessity.

MODIFIER A word, **phrase**, or **clause** that describes or specifies something about another word, phrase, or clause (*a long, informative speech; an intellectually demanding presentation; the actors spoke in union*).

NARRATE, NARRATION, NARRATIVE A **strategy** for presenting information as a story, for telling what happened. It is a pattern most often associated with fiction, but it shows up in all kinds of

writing. When used in an essay, a **report**, or another academic **genre,** a narrative must support a point, not merely tell an interesting story for its own sake. It must also present events in some kind of sequence and include only pertinent detail. Sometimes narrative serves as the **organizing** principle for a whole text. *See also* **literacy narrative.**

NARRATOR/SPEAKER The character or person who tells the story.

NOUN A word that refers to a person, place, animal, thing, or idea (*director, Stephen King, forest, Amazon River, tree frog, notebook, democracy*).

OBJECT A word or phrase that follows a **preposition** or receives the action of a **verb.** In the sentence *I handed him the mail that was on the table, him* is the indirect object and *mail* is the direct object of the verb *handed; table* is the object of the preposition *on.*

ORGANIZING Arranging parts of a text so that the text as a whole has **coherence.** The text may use one **strategy** throughout or may combine several strategies to create a suitable organization.

OUTLINING A process for **generating ideas and text** or for examining a text. An *informal outline* simply lists ideas and then numbers them in the order that they will appear; a *working outline* distinguishes support from main ideas by indenting the former; a *formal outline* is arranged as a series of headings and indented subheadings, each on a separate line, with letters and numerals indicating relative levels of importance.

PARAPHRASING Rewording a text in about the same number of words but without using the word order or sentence structure of the original. A paraphrase is generally used when you want to include the details of a passage but do not need to quote it word for word. Like a quotation, a paraphrase requires documentation.

PASSIVE VOICE A grammatical construction in which the object of an action becomes the grammatical subject: *The baseball was hit by the boy. See also* active voice.

PATHOS A mode of persuasion that appeals to the audience's emotions.

PERSONAL ESSAY A genre of writing that tells about a personal experience. Key Features: well-told story • vivid detail • indication of the narrative's significance.

PERSUADE, PERSUASION, PERSUASIVE In argument, to attempt to motivate your reader to behave in a specific way. Persuading may differ from convincing in that convincing is designed to get the reader to agree, while persuading is designed to get the reader to act.

PERSUASIVE ESSAY A genre of writing in which the writer presents an argument and attempts to **convince** the reader to agree and then **persuade** the reader to act upon its conclusions. Key Features: logical reasoning • necessary background • convincing **evidence**.

PHRASE A group of words that lacks a subject, a **verb**, or both.

PLAGIARISM Using another person's words, syntax, or ideas without giving appropriate credit and **documentation**. Plagiarism is a serious breach of ethics.

PLOT/STRUCTURE The arrangement of the action. Traditionally, a plot has five parts: **exposition, rising action, climax, falling action,** and **dénouement.**

POINT OF VIEW A position from which something is considered.

PORTFOLIO A collection of writing selected by a writer to show his or her work, sometimes including a statement assessing the work and explaining what it demonstrates.

POSITION A statement that asserts a belief or **claim**. In an **argument**, a position needs to be stated in a **thesis** or clearly implied, and requires support with **reasons** and **evidence**.

POST HOC, ERGO PROPTER HOC After this, therefore because of this (Latin); also called **faulty causality**. A **fallacy** of assuming that the first of two events causes the second.

PREDICATE In a sentence or **clause**, the **verb** and the words that tell more about the verb—its **complements**, **modifiers**, and **objects**. In the sentence *Mario forcefully stated his opinion*, the predicate is *forcefully stated his opinion*.

PREPOSITION A word or group of words that tells about the relationship of a **noun** or **pronoun** to another part of the sentence. Some common prepositions are *after, at, because of, before, in, on, on top of, under, until, with*, and *without*.

PRIMARY SOURCE A source such as a literary work, historical document, work of art, or performance that a researcher examines firsthand. Primary sources also include experiments and **field research**. In writing about the Revolutionary War, a researcher would likely consider the Declaration of Independence a primary source and a textbook's description of the writing of the document a **secondary source**.

PROCESS In writing, a series of actions that may include **generating ideas and text, drafting, revising, editing**, and **proofreading** a text. *See also* **process analysis**.

PROCESS ANALYSIS A **strategy** for telling how something is done or how to do something. Sometimes an analysis of a process serves as the **organizing** principle for a whole text.

PROFILE A **genre** of writing that presents an engaging portrait of a person, place, or event based on firsthand **field research**. Key Features: interesting subject • necessary background • distinctive angle • firsthand account • engaging details.

PRONOUN A word that takes the place of a **noun** or functions the way a noun does.

PROOFREADING The final **process** in writing, when a writer checks for correct spelling and punctuation as well as for page order, any missing copy, and the consistent use of typefaces and fonts. *See also* **editing, revising**, and **rewriting**.

PROPOSAL A **genre** of writing that argues for a solution to a problem or suggests some action. *See also* **topic proposal**. Key Features: well-defined problem • recommended solution • answers to anticipated questions • call to action • appropriate **tone**.

PURPOSE A writer's goal: for example, to explore, to express oneself, to entertain, to demonstrate learning, to inform, or to persuade. Purpose is one element of the **rhetorical situation**.

QUESTIONING A **process** of generating **ideas and text** about a topic—asking, for example, *what, who, when, where, how*, and *why*, or other questions.

QUOTATION Someone's words repeated exactly as they were spoken or written. Quotation is most effective when the wording is worth repeating or makes a point so well that no rewording will do it justice, or when a writer wants to cite someone's exact words or quote someone whose opinions disagree with others. Quotations need to be acknowledged with **documentation**.

REASON A statement supporting a **claim** or **position**. A reason, in turn, requires its own **support**.

REFERENCES (APA) The list of sources at the end of a text prepared **APA style**.

REFLECTION A **genre** of writing that presents a writer's thoughtful, personal exploration of a subject. Key Features: topic intriguing to the writer • some kind of structure • specific details • speculative **tone**.

RELATIVE PRONOUN A **pronoun** such as *that, which, who, whoever, whom*, and *whomever* that connects a **subordinate clause** to a sentence: *The professor who gave the lecture is my adviser.*

REPORTING A **genre** of writing that presents information as objectively as possible to inform readers about a subject. *See also* **lab report, journalistic narrative**. Key Features: tightly focused **topic** • accurate, well-researched information • various **writing strategies** • clear **definitions** • appropriate **design**.

RESEARCH The practice of investigating sources, whether written, oral, or visual, to advance knowledge and to provide support for a writer's **claim**. *See also* **documented essay**.

RESPOND, RESPONDING (TO WRITING), RESPONSE A process of writing in which a reader responds to a writer's work by giving his or her thoughts about the writer's title, beginning, clarity of **thesis**, support and **documentation**, **organization**, **stance**, treatment of the **audience**, achievement of **purpose**, handling of the **genre**, ending, and other matters.

RÉSUMÉ A **genre** of writing that summarizes someone's academic and employment history, generally written to submit to potential employers. **Design** and word choice depend on whether a résumé is submitted as a print document or in an electronic or scannable form. Key Features: organization that suits goals and experience • succinctness • design that highlights key information (print) or that uses only one typeface (scannable).

REVISE, REVISION The process of making substantive changes, including additions and cuts, to a draft so that it contains all the necessary information in an appropriate organization. During revision, a writer generally moves from whole-text issues to details with the goals of sharpening the focus and strengthening the argument.

REWRITING A process of composing a new draft from another perspective—from a different point of view, audience, stance, genre, medium, sequence, and so on.

RHETORIC The "art, practice, and study of (ethical) human communication" (Andrea Lunsford). Rhetoric can but doesn't necessarily incorporate the art of persuasion; in the field of composition, the term is not typically used in the sense of insincere or inflated language.

RHETORICAL QUESTION A question asked merely for effect with no answer expected: *What were you thinking?*

RHETORICAL SITUATION The context within which writing or other communication takes place, including **purpose, audience, genre, stance,** and **media/design.**

RISING ACTION The second of the five parts of **plot** structure, in which events complicate the situation that existed at the beginning of a work, intensifying the **conflict** or introducing new conflict.

ROGERIAN ARGUMENT A method of argument, introduced by psychologist Carl Rogers, based on finding common ground on all sides of an issue before stating one's own **position.**

SATIRE A **genre** of writing in which the writer holds up human failings to ridicule and censure. Key Features:

irony • sarcasm • **purpose** of improving the reader.

SECONDARY SOURCE An **analysis** or **interpretation** of a **primary source.** In writing about the Revolutionary War, a researcher would likely consider the Declaration of Independence a **primary source** and a textbook's description of writing of the document a secondary source.

SETTING The time and place of the action in a piece of writing.

SIGNAL PHRASE A phrase used to attribute **quoted, paraphrased,** or **summarized** material to a source, as in *she said* or *he claimed.*

SIMILE A figure of speech that compares two items using *like* or *as*: "*Still we live meanly, like ants*" (Henry David Thoreau, *Walden*), "*The Wind begun to knead the Grass—/As Women do a Dough—*" (Emily Dickinson).

SLIPPERY SLOPE A **fallacy** that asserts, without **evidence,** that one event will lead to a series of other events that will culminate in a cataclysm.

SPEAKER The person, not necessarily the author, who is the **voice** of a piece of writing.

STANCE A writer's or speaker's attitude toward his or her subject as conveyed through the **tone** and word choice.

STRATEGY A pattern for **organizing** text to analyze **cause and effect, classify and divide, compare and contrast, define, describe, explain a process, narrate,** and so on.

STEREOTYPE A characterization based on the conscious or unconscious assumption that a particular aspect—such as gender, age, ethnic or national identity, religion, occupation, and marital status—is predictably accompanied by certain **character** traits, actions, even values.

STREAM OF CONSCIOUSNESS A method of writing in which the writer conveys the thoughts and feelings of the speaker or a character through a continuous flow of conscious experience; an interior monologue.

STYLE (1) In writing, the arrangement of sentences, phrases, words, and punctuation to achieve a desired effect; (2) the rules of capitalization, punctuation, and so on recommended for the **documentation** of a source.

SUBJECT A word or word group, usually including at least one **noun or pronoun** plus its **modifiers,** that tells who or what a sentence or **clause** is about. In the sentence *An increasingly frustrated group of commuters waited for the late bus,* the subject is *An increasingly frustrated group of commuters.*

SUBORDINATE CLAUSE A **clause,** containing a subject and a verb, that contains a subordinating word and therefore cannot stand alone as a sentence: *He wheezes <u>when he exercises</u>. My roommate, <u>who was a physics major</u>, tutors high school students in science.*

SUMMARY A condensation of a text into a briefer but still faithful version in lieu of a **paraphrase** or a **quotation.**

SUMMARY-RESPONSE A **genre** of writing in which the writer or speaker presents both a **summary** of a text or texts and **responds** to the text. Key Features: brief summary of the text • highlights of major points of the text • **evaluation** of the text.

SYMBOL A person, place, thing, event, or pattern in a literary work that designates itself and at the same time figuratively represents or "stands for" something else. Often the thing or idea represented is more abstract or general; the symbol, more concrete and particular.

SYNTHESIZING IDEAS A way of generating new information or supporting a new perspective by bringing together ideas and information from two or more sources.

TEXTUAL ANALYSIS A **genre** of writing in which a writer looks at what a text says and how it says it. *See also* **analysis** and **literary analysis.** Key Features:

summary of the text • attention to context • clear **interpretation** • reasonable support for your conclusions.

THEME (1) The central or dominant idea or concern of a work; (2) the statement a poem makes about its subject.

THESIS A **claim** or statement of a writer's **position** or main point.

TONE A writer's or speaker's attitude toward his or her readers and subject. A writer's tone reflects his or her **stance** and may be formal or informal, optimistic or pessimistic, playful, ironic, and so on.

TOPIC The subject of a piece of writing; what a text is about.

TOPIC PROPOSAL A statement of intent to examine a topic; also called a proposal **abstract**. Some instructors require a topic proposal in order to assess the feasibility of the writing project that a student has in mind. Key Features: concise discussion of the subject • clear statement of the intended focus • rationale for choosing the subject • mention of resources.

TOPIC SENTENCE A sentence, usually the first in a paragraph, that encapsulates what that paragraph is about. The topic sentence often includes a claim that will be supported in the paragraph.

TOULMIN ARGUMENT A six-part method of analyzing the structure of **arguments** formulated by British philosopher Stephen Toulmin. The elements of this model include the **claim**, the grounds, the warrant, the backing, the qualifier, and the rebuttal.

TRANSITIONS Words or **phrases** used to make clear the connection between ideas and text.

VANTAGE POINT The position or standpoint from which a writer **describes** something.

VERB A word or a group of words that conveys an action (*dance, determine, observe*) or a state of being (*be, seem*) and is an essential element of a sentence or **clause**.

VOICE The acknowledged or unacknowledged source of a piece of writing's words; the speaker; the "person" telling the story.

WORKS-CITED LIST (MLA) At the end of a researched text prepared MLA style, the list of all the sources cited in the text, with full bibliographic information.

JAMES L. HARPER JR. { *You're Here!*

JAMES L. HARPER JR., *a staff sergeant in the U.S. Air Force, took this photo on September 13, 2008, the day that Hurricane Ike struck the Gulf Coast of the United States. The image shows a resident of Galveston, Texas—a shoreline community that was ravaged during the Category 2 hurricane—hugging Lopaka Mounts, a search-and-rescue specialist with the Air Force. Mounts was on a mission to find survivors of Ike, an endeavor that Texas governor Rick Perry's office called the largest search-and-rescue operation ever conducted in Texas. There are many ways to approach this image rhetorically: as a cause-and-effect text, for instance, or a memoir, or a profile of an Air Force officer. What is the most useful way to approach this image?*